SO-AZP-146

Copyright © 1989, 1993 Modern Publishing, a division of Unisystems, Inc.

Deinonychus
© 1984 Rourke Enterprises, Inc.
Copyright © 1984 Martspress Ltd., Nork Way Banstead, Surrey,
SM7 1PB

Anatosaurus; Pachycephalosaurus; Psittacosaurus;
Rutiodon; Scolosaurus; Spinosaurus
© 1989 Rourke Enterprises, Inc.
The Dinosaur Dictionary (edited version)
© 1988 Rourke Enterprises, Inc.

®—Honey Bear Books is a trademark owned by Honey Bear
Productions, Inc., and is registered in the U.S. Patent and
Trademark Office.

Introduction by Michael Teitelbaum
Revised text for bindup edition of Terms to Remember compiled
by Michael Teitelbaum
Cover art, endsheet art and title page art by Lee Ann Leigh
*Line illustrations by Chris Simms, **Tim Madden

All Rights Reserved

No part of this book may be reproduced or copied in any
format without written permission from the publisher.

Printed in Italy

COLOSSAL
BOOK OF DINOSAURS

Featuring:
THE DINOSAUR DICTIONARY

Modern Publishing
A Division of Unisystems, Inc.
New York, New York 10022

Printed in Italy

Introduction

The first dinosaur fossils were found approximately 100 years ago. Ever since their discovery, human beings have been fascinated by the prehistoric inhabitants of Earth who lived millions of years ago!

Everyday, archeologists and paleontologists continue to uncover new and exciting information about dinosaurs, and man has learned a great deal about these strange and wonderful creatures. Many questions, however, remain unanswered. How did these huge monsters evolve from the simple reptiles that preceded them? How did they hunt? How did they raise their young? What caused the sudden extinction of the many members and branches of this prehistoric "family."

During the Mesozoic Era—a time period also called "The Age of Dinosaurs"—an astounding variety of creatures roamed Earth. Man has discovered evidence of huge beasts, who weighed several tons apiece; small, quick animals, who ran through prehistoric forests; flying reptiles, who soared through the sky; and fierce predators, who hunted and killed other creatures for food.

This book provides a fascinating look into the Age of Dinosaurs. Adventure-filled stories and exciting, full-color illustrations offer true-to-life accounts of several dinosaurs' daily lives. The "Facts About Dinosaurs" section contains added, concise information about these amazing creatures.

A "Dinosaur Dictionary" is included in this volume so that readers may easily discover pertinent facts about their favorite Sauropod, Ceratopsian, or Pterosaur.

Prepare for a wonderful journey, back in time, to an Earth ruled by the incredible dinosaurs.

Table of Contents

Introduction 7
Table of Contents 9
What is a Dinosaur? 10
The Age of Dinosaurs 12
Dinosaur Sizes 14
Anatosaurus 17
Deinonychus 37
Pachycephalosaurus 57
Psittacosaurus 77
Rutiodon 97
Scolosaurus 117
Spinosaurus 137
Facts About Dinosaurs 156
Dinosaur Dictionary 170
Terms to Remember 236

WHAT IS A DINOSAUR?

TYPES OF DINOSAUR

There were many types of dinosaur but among the most famous was the family of sauropods. These were large, four-footed animals with small heads, long necks, large bodies, and long tails. They had quite small brains with a special nerve box in their hip to control the tail and back legs.

Heavily armored dinosaurs like this "node-lizard" ankylosaur were built for protection and combat. They walked on all fours and ate plants. Some were armed with large bony clubs at the end of the tail. Others just had side and back armor. Several types had spikes and plates.

Probably the most feared dinosaurs of all were the flesh-eating carnosaurs like *Daspletosaurus*. They walked erect on two legs; most had very small arms and weighed up to 7 tons. They could move quickly and would eat dead animals as well as kill other dinosaurs for food. All had large fangs.

DINOSAUR GROUPS

Whichever family a dinosaur belonged to it was in one of two groups. The groups were distinguished by the way their hip bones were arranged. These bones are called the ilium, the ischium and the pubis. Saurischian (lizard-hip) dinosaurs had a hip bone arrangement like that seen in the drawing on the right.

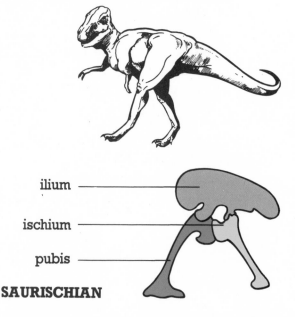

ilium

ischium

pubis

SAURISCHIAN

Ornithischian dinosaurs had the hip arrangement shown in the drawing on the left. Here, the pubis lies back along the ischium. Later, some dinosaurs had a different pubic bone shaped to point more forward than previous types and is shown here jutting beyond the ilium. All ornithischians were plant eaters.

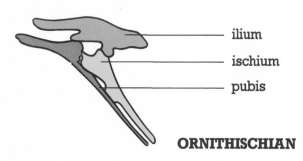

ilium

ischium

pubis

ORNITHISCHIAN

THE DINOSAUR WALK

The dinosaur was distinguished by the way its legs were attached to its hips. In the drawings below you can see the squat arrangement of a lizard, the semi-raised posture of a crocodile and the fully developed structure of a mammal or a dinosaur. The way the hip joints developed is also shown. We must not think of dinosaurs as primitive. They were highly developed.

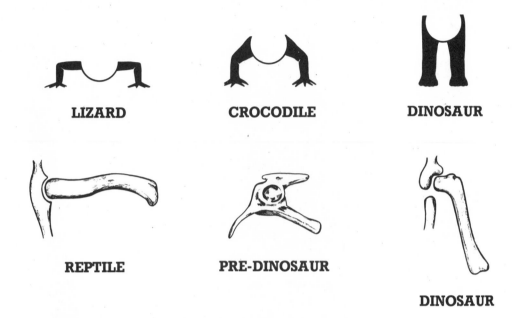

LIZARD   CROCODILE   DINOSAUR

REPTILE   PRE-DINOSAUR

DINOSAUR

DINOSAUR FEET

Some dinosaurs walked on their toes, like *Ceratosaurus* whose leg and foot is shown in the left-hand drawing below. Other dinosaur feet, like those of *Apatosaurus* at bottom right, were adapted for carrying great weights across firm ground. It is wrong to think of giant sauropods like these wallowing in marshy swamps. Studies show they would have become hopelessly bogged down!

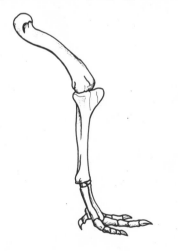

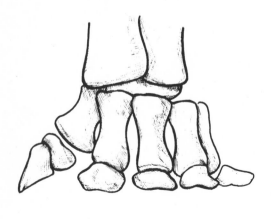

THE AGE OF THE DINOSAURS

SAURISCHIAN (LIZARD-HIP)

Dinosaurs of this type were found all over the world and lived from the middle of the Triassic period to the end of the Cretaceous. They were both meat and plant eaters, had clawed feet and included the families of sauropods (with five toes like modern lizards), carnosaurs (bipedal meat eaters) and coelurosaurs (similar to carnosaurs but with hollow bones, large brains and possibly warm blooded). Reptiles and crocodiles are shown for comparison.

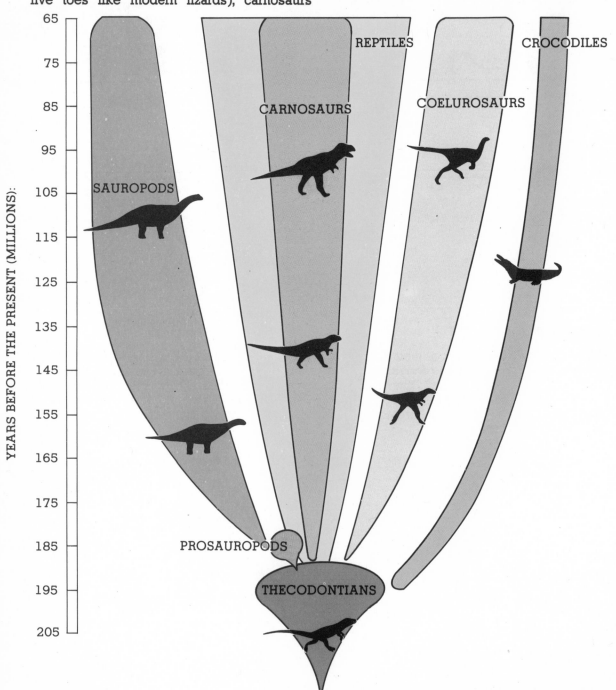

YEARS BEFORE THE PRESENT (MILLIONS):

65
75
85
95
105
115
125
135
145
155
165
175
185
195
205

REPTILES

CROCODILES

CARNOSAURS

COELUROSAURS

SAUROPODS

PROSAUROPODS

THECODONTIANS

ORNITHISCHIAN (BIRD-HIP)

These dinosaurs had hoofed toes, ate plants and most had beaked mouths. Some, like the stegosaurs and the ankylosaurs, had protective armor. Ornithopods were thought to have bird-like feet and ran with tails outstretched for balance. Pterosaurs were not true birds.

Modern birds are thought to have come from Saurischian Coelurosaurs. The age of the birds and mammals are shown for comparison. Like reptiles and crocodiles, they have survived to the present.

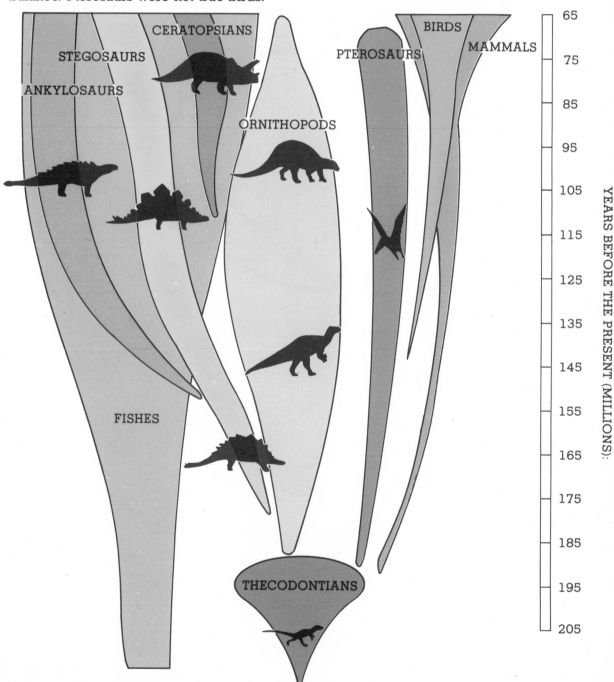

CERATOPSIANS

STEGOSAURS

ANKYLOSAURS

ORNITHOPODS

PTEROSAURS

BIRDS

MAMMALS

FISHES

THECODONTIANS

YEARS BEFORE THE PRESENT (MILLIONS):

65
75
85
95
105
115
125
135
145
155
165
175
185
195
205

13

DINOSAUR SIZES

PLATEOSAURUS

DASPLETOSAURUS

COELURUS

STEGOSAURUS

TRICERATOPS

COMPSOGNATHUS

From the giant Diplodocus to the tiny Compsognathus, dinosaurs came in all shapes and sizes. Here dinosaurs are compared with modern animals like the elephant, the hippopotamus, the rhinoceros, the giraffe, the dog and man. Compare the size of Tyrannosaurus with a rhinoceros and see how Triceratops would have looked to a man!

Many dinosaurs, like Coelurus, were fast, nimble and hard to catch. Others, like Diplodocus, were slow, lumbering animals rather like the modern elephant. Stegosaurus, like the rhinoceros, was well protected and could probably run quite fast too. What a strange sight it would be if all these animals could really be seen around today!

HIPPOPOTAMUS

ELEPHANT

TYRANNOSAURUS

RHINOCEROS

DIPLODOCUS

GIRAFFE

MAN

DOG

Quetzalcoatlus

Parasaurolophus

Deinosuchus

Corythosaurus

Spinosaurus

Oviraptor

16

Anatosaurus

Written by David White
Illustrated by Pam Mara

Pachycephalosaurus

Anatosaurus

Struthiomimus

Scolosaurus

Rutiodon

Psittacosaurus

As the sun filtered through the trees of the forest, Anatosaurus awoke. Nearby lay the rest of the herd. Anatosaurus sniffed the morning air, and smelled the scent of flowers at the forest edge. He was hungry and thirsty.

He stood on his hind legs, using his great tail to balance himself, and bit off the branch of an oak. Anatosaurus chewed slowly. His strong teeth could grind any foliage, even pine needles, to make a meal that he could digest. He browsed quietly among the branches of the tree. The forest was his home and his source of food. In it, he could find all the leaves and fruit he wanted.

When he was young, Anatosaurus lived near the water. His mother hatched her eggs on the shore of a lake, so that the hatchlings could run to the water whenever there was danger. Then he had lived on water weeds, sucking them up from the water.

When he grew older and his teeth became
strong, he moved away from the lake and into the
forest. There was always plenty to eat. The forest
contained every kind of tree – pines and firs, oaks, ash,
poplars, sycamores, willows, maples, and birch.

After a morning of grazing, Anatosaurus lay
down and dozed in the midday heat. He did not sleep,
however. There was always the danger of attack by
other animals, especially the fierce meat-eaters.

Luckily, Anatosaurus had sharp eyes and good
hearing. Most important of all, he had a keen sense of
smell. While it was still far away, he could smell the
scent of another animal in the wind. This gave him
plenty of warning.

Today, though, there was no wind. The forest was hot and still. Anatosaurus could hear the grunting of the herd as it browsed contentedly in the heat. Suddenly, the grunting changed to a loud croaking. Something had frightened the herd. Animals began to run off through the trees. Anatosaurus got up on his hind legs. He could run fastest this way.

Then the cause of all the panic burst into sight. It was Deinonychus, known as "terrible claw". Deinonychus was only a small animal, but his sickle-like claw made him a fearsome opponent. With his claw, he could wound and even kill animals much larger than himself.

Anatosaurus was no match for Deinonychus, so he did the only thing he could. He ran. He ran through the dense undergrowth of shrubs and small trees toward the lake. He knew instinctively that the water would protect him.

Anatosaurus was as suited to the water as to the land. He had webbed feet and a long flat-sided tail to help him swim fast. Once he reached the lake, he knew he would be safe.

As he ran, he could hear Deinonychus behind him. He looked anxiously for a sign of the lake. With his great weight, Anatosaurus was beginning to get tired. If he stopped for breath, he knew that Deinonychus would be on his back, tearing at him with his terrible sickle-claw.

Suddenly, the lake came into view. Anatosaurus bounded across the shore and plunged into the water. He swam away from the land with a few powerful sweeps of his tail. Deinonychus could only stand at the water's edge and watch his prey escape. Then he turned away and loped off in search of other prey.

Afterwards, Anatosaurus returned to the shore. The lakeside was now calm and peaceful. Palaeotringa, long-legged wading birds, probed the sand for shellfish and worms. Plegadornis stood at the water's edge, watching for frogs and water beetles.

Graculavus, who had been diving for fish, shook his wings dry as he perched on a rock by the lake.

Anatosaurus found plenty of food around the lakeside. He ate pistia, or water lettuce, and trapa, water chestnut. If he waded into the lake, he could sample some salvinia, a floating fern.

As Anatosaurus took his pick of the succulent plants, a herd of Brachylophosaurs wandered onto the shore. They were harmless, plant-eating creatures like himself. Yet suddenly, Anatosaurus heard the harsh clash of bone against bone, as Brachylophosaurus battled with Brachylophosaurus.

It was a trial of strength, rather than a fight. One of the younger members of the herd had challenged the herd leader to a contest. The two animals stood face to face. Then they pressed their face plates, made of solid bone, against each other. The winner was the one who forced the other to give way. He could then become the leader of the herd.

Anatosaurus stopped browsing among the greenery to watch the contest. At first, it looked as though the young Brachylophosaurus would win. Then the experience of the leader began to tell. The older Brachylophosaurus started to push the younger one back.

Just as it seemed that the leader would win, a terrifying roar sent the birds of the lake flying into the air. Out of the forest stalked Tyrannosaurus. He saw the herd of Brachylophosaurs and broke into a run. The great creature took short, awkward steps, giving the herd time to scatter. Anatosaurus fled with them.

Tyrannosaurus watched the herd scattering in front of him. He was looking for the weakest and the slowest animal. Finally, he made his move, darting in among the Brachylophosaurs. Anatosaurus saw his chance and ran for the edge of the forest.

He looked back. Tyrannosaurus stood over a
Brachylophosaurus, tearing at it with his vicious teeth.
The rest of the herd had escaped, and so had Anatosaurus.

In the late afternoon, Anatosaurus rejoined his
own herd in the oak forest. He found them browsing
peacefully. Anatosaurus was tired and hungry by now.
He reached up to the branches of an oak tree and began
to eat. The running had tired him. Soon he lay down,
curled up his great body in the forest undergrowth, and
slept. The light faded slowly in the forest.

Rhamphorhynchus

Pteranodon

Pterodactyl

Ankylosaurus

Dimetrodon

Iguanodon

Tricondon

36

Deinonychus

Written by Rupert Oliver
Illustrated by Roger Payne

Archaeopteryx

Ichthyosaurus

Plesiosaurus

Deinonychus

Nothosaurus

Deinonychus shifted his position to make himself more comfortable. A sharp twig had been digging into his ribs. He had been resting in the shade of the tree for several hours now.

Idly, he raised his great claw and scratched himself behind the ear. The terrible heat of the noon sun was too strong for Deinonychus, but it was beginning to cool down now. His ear still itched. Deinonychus lifted his foot up again and scratched himself more vigorously. This time he disturbed a large insect which flew away. It had been biting him and sucking his blood. Deinonychus was comfortable now and he dozed off again. As he dozed a butterfly flew past on its colorful wings. Deinonychus did not like the hot weather but it suited the insects.

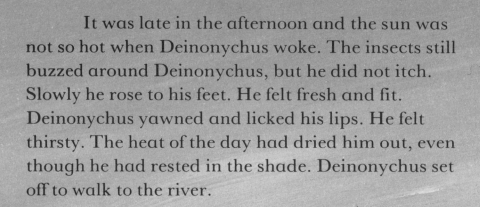

It was late in the afternoon and the sun was not so hot when Deinonychus woke. The insects still buzzed around Deinonychus, but he did not itch. Slowly he rose to his feet. He felt fresh and fit. Deinonychus yawned and licked his lips. He felt thirsty. The heat of the day had dried him out, even though he had rested in the shade. Deinonychus set off to walk to the river.

Following a well-used track between the trees and bushes, Deinonychus reached the water's edge. The river was full of fresh, cool water. The arrival of Deinonychus disturbed a pair of turtles who splashed back into the safety of the river.

Deinonychus walked out across the mud flats to the water. He bent down to drink. Suddenly, the whole water surface seemed to explode with spray and foam right at the feet of Deinonychus. In sudden fear, Deinonychus stepped back as a vicious pair of jaws snapped shut, inches from his leg. Out of the flying water emerged the head and body of a crocodile. It had been lying in shallow water waiting. Deinonychus had walked right into the trap.

Quickly, Deinonychus scrambled back across the mud to the dry land. The crocodile did not follow Deinonychus. It preferred to sink back into the water and wait for another animal to come to drink.

Deinonychus ran into the trees lining the river. He had not completely satisfied his thirst, but he did not want to go back to the river if the crocodile was still there. Perhaps if he went to another part of the river there would be no crocodiles.

Suddenly, Deinonychus heard a distant crash. He stood still. Then another crash sounded out, much nearer. Now Deinonychus could hear heavy footsteps and the sound of smashing branches. Something was coming and whatever it was, it was very large. Deinonychus was worried that it was a meat-eater. It would be safest to hide.

Deinonychus pushed his way into a thick bush and waited. The sound of footsteps came closer and closer and then Deinonychus could see a looming bulk as the creature came into sight. Deinonychus need not have worried. The newcomer was a Tenontosaurus. This dinosaur was big, but it ate plants and was no danger to Deinonychus.

When it had gone Deinonychus came out of hiding and looked around. The Tenontosaurus had left a path of flattened and broken vegetation behind it as it smashed a way through the forest. Deinonychus decided to follow the path. It would be easier than picking his own route.

Deinonychus walked along the tracks of the Tenontosaurus until he reached the edge of the forest. Instead of finding himself at a river, Deinonychus was at the edge of a wide plain. He could see for miles across the landscape. On the plain was a group of animals. When Deinonychus saw what they were he felt his stomach rumbling. They were Psittacosaurs. Deinonychus suddenly felt very hungry.

Deinonychus knew that he would have to be very careful when hunting the Psittacosaurs. If they saw him they would run away and Deinonychus would have to go hungry.

Deinonychus walked out on to the plain as if he had not seen the Psittacosaurs. He did not walk straight toward them. He walked toward a small clump of trees to one side. One Psittacosaurus looked up from its feeding to watch the Deinonychus. When it saw that the Deinonychus was not coming toward it, the Psittacosaurus continued eating.

Using the trees as cover, Deinonychus was able to get close to the Psittacosaurs without being seen. As soon as he left the trees and moved toward the plant-eaters he was seen. One of the Psittacosaurs gave a bellow of alarm and started to run. The other Psittacosaurs heard the cry and also began to run. If he was to stand any chance of a meal, Deinonychus too, had to run. The chase had begun.

49

Using his long legs Deinonychus bounded after the retreating Psittacosaurs. One of the plant-eaters was slower than the others. Perhaps he was old or ill, either way he would be the easiest to catch. Deinonychus decided to chase him. Across the plain the two dinosaurs raced. Their feet kicked up the dust as they ran.

Deinonychus was gaining on the Psittacosaurus. Then it stumbled. Now it stood no chance against Deinonychus. Deinonychus leapt high into the air. He brought his hind legs up under his body and raised his great claws. He had judged the leap perfectly. Deinonychus landed right on top of the Psittacosaurus. His huge, sickle-shaped claws ripped deep into the plant-eater. The Psittacosaurus gave a roar of pain and tried to escape, but Deinonychus was hungry and plunged his terrible claws into the soft body of the Psittacosaurus again and again. Within seconds it was all over and the Psittacosaurus lay dead at the feet of Deinonychus.

Deinonychus climbed off the still body of the Psittacosaurus. The long chase had made him breathless. Then he began to eat. He bent down and tore great mouthfuls of meat from the carcass.

As Deinonychus began to eat he saw a pair of small Coelurosaurs standing nearby. Deinonychus roared at them angrily, but they did not move away. Deinonychus continued eating. While he was still eating, one of the Coelurosaurs dashed in and grabbed a mouthful of meat. Deinonychus left the body of the Psittacosaurus when he was full. Then both the Coelurosaurs dashed in and began to eat.

As Deinonychus moved away the sun was setting. He felt much better with a full stomach and moved off to find somewhere to rest for the night. Behind him the small animals continued to squabble over pieces of meat, but the sounds of their fight faded as Deinonychus moved away. In the shelter of some bushes Deinonychus found a soft patch of ferns to lie on. He settled down and closed his eyes. It had been a tiring day and Deinonychus was very tired. Soon he was fast asleep.

Quetzalcoatlus

Parasaurolophus

Deinosuchus

Corythosaurus

Oviraptor

56 Spinosaurus

Pachycephalosaurus

Written by Frances Swann
Illustrated by Pam Mara

Pachycephalosaurus

Anatosaurus

Struthiomimus

Scolosaurus

Rutiodon

Psittacosaurus

It was early morning when Pachycephalosaurus awoke. The air was hot, dry and still.

A little way off, a couple of one-year-old males were playfighting. Their noise disturbed the others, and slowly the rest of Pachycephalosaurus' small herd began to stir. The herd had slept in the shelter of a huge overhanging rock on the treeless hillside. It was the dry season. Soon the sun would rise higher, and even in the shadow of the rock it would be uncomfortably hot.

The herd was hungry. They assembled gradually behind Pachycephalosaurus. Slowly they moved down the hillside in search of fresh vegetation and shade.

59

Pachycephalosaurus felt restless. He was the oldest, largest, and strongest of the males. Therefore, he was the dominant male and the herd leader. This was the mating season, a time when other males would challenge his position. So far he had always won. Pachycephalosaurus knew that one day the outcome would be different, and he would lose his herd to a younger male.

Pachycephalosaurus called his herd in closer. The descent was steep and the ground hard and stony. A Pterosaur flew low over the group. Pachycephalosaurus felt a rush of warm air from its leathery wings. He watched as it glided down toward the valley.

Over the green and yellow treetops he could see the thin blue line of the river. A vast flood plain lay beyond, and the hazy line of a mountain range lay beyond that.

A sudden crack of thunder frightened the herd. They bunched closer together. A lizard darted back into the rocks. The herd quickened its pace.

The descent was less steep now, and the vegetation thicker. The herd stopped to feed on some bushes. Pachycephalosaurus chewed the leaves, but remained watchful. Another clap of thunder shook the valley. Pachycephalosaurus turned. To his horror he saw another Pachycephalosaurus herd standing absolutely still, watching him. In front was a powerful male, his challenging posture unmistakable.

The two males approached each other menacingly, watched by their herds. As the distance between them lessened, both males adopted a butting posture. Heads down, with backs and tails held in a stiff, straight line, they ran at each other.

Their heads met with a dull thud. They retreated and charged at each other again and again. Suddenly the other male withdrew, panting with exhaustion. Pachycephalosaurus had won!

To prove his victory, Pachycephalosaurus chased the challenger and his herd into the thicket of katsura trees. Pachycephalosaurus was shaken, but unhurt.

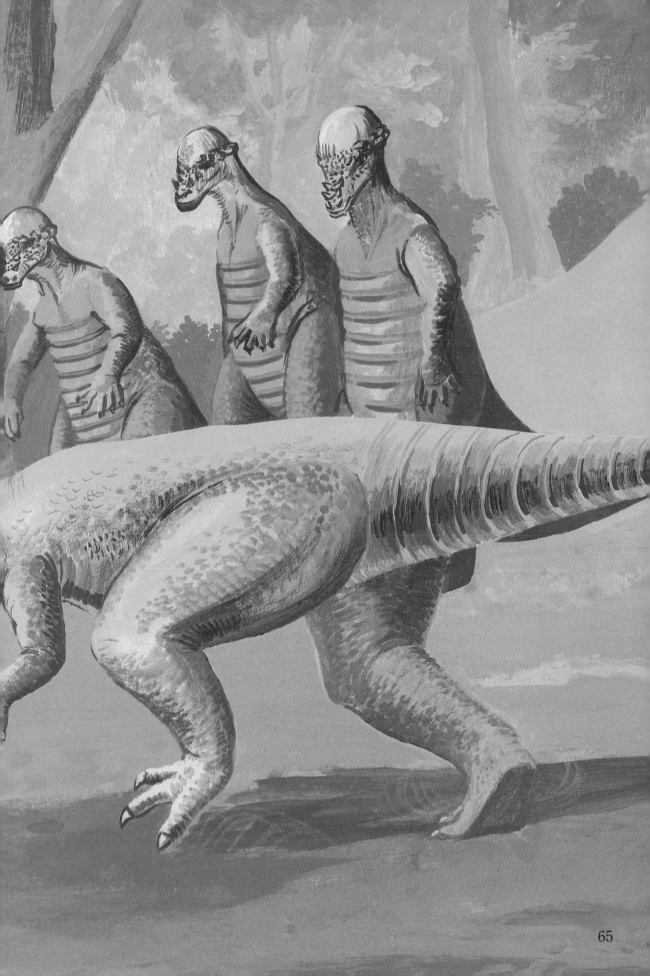

Pachycephalosaurus needed to get his breath back, so the herd moved slowly into the shade of the trees.

The ground was covered with oval yellow katsura leaves. A shrew-like mammal darted out to catch a beetle, and a line of ants swarmed up the trunk of a breadfruit tree. All seemed still.

The herd moved forward. Above them rose the tall silvery bark and the lime green canopy of sycamore trees. A sudden commotion brought the herd to a halt.

Through the trees they could see two male Chasmorsaurs locked in battle. The horns on their great frilled heads clashed together as they pushed and swayed violently.

The Chasmosaurs were intent on their contest and the herd passed unnoticed.

Pachycephalosaurus grew uneasy as the day continued. A strange smell was in the air. A pair of Stenonychosaurs sprinted back and forth catching insects. They seemed unbothered.

The smell grew stronger and stronger. Smoke! Pachycephalosaurus was filled with terror. The herd's territory was on the hillside, but the fire had them trapped. Panic stricken, the herd fled deeper into the trees, heading instinctively for the river.

They ran headlong through the thick undergrowth, almost trampling a Panoplosaurus as it lay clutching the ground with alarm.

The smoke was all around them now and the whole forest seemed on the move. The ground shook as a herd of Triceratops charged blindly past them. Small mammals raced across the forest floor, and birds flew wildly above them.

A fleet-footed Struthiomimus raced by, disappearing into the distance. The herd was beginning to tire. Pachycephalosaurus was a large animal and not used to running so far, but terror and panic drove him.

At last the air grew clearer and Pachycephalosaurus could breathe more easily. They were leaving the fire behind.

The herd did not stop until they reached the dry sandy land by the river. Here they drank and rested, in the cover of the tall rushes under the redwood trees.

It was late afternoon before Pachycephalosaurus led his herd out along the river. The air was cooler, sun sparkled on the water, and all along the bank turtles plopped back into the river as the herd passed.

Several half-submerged crocodiles lay in the shallow water at the river's edge. Suddenly, one stood up. With a fast, zig-zagging pace, he made for a clump of tall rushes.

The herd stopped as the dark shape of an angry female Parasaurolophus rose from her nest. She had been sitting on her eggs. Her threatening posture, and her size were too much for the crocodile. It turned back and slid quietly into the river.

Pachycephalosaurus had no wish to anger the Parasaurolophus any further. He led his herd around her nest site, and on through the rushes.

As they rounded the next bend there was a sudden explosion of sound. A deafening mixture of bellows, roars, and splashes filled the air. The herd came to an abrupt halt. Pachycephalosaurus looked wildly about him for the source of the noise.

On the far bank of the river a pack of Dromaeosaurs had killed a Coryothsaurus. Quarrelling among themselves, they were already tearing at their kill.

Thundering toward them was a massive Tyrannosaurus. It roared defiantly, hoping to scatter the Dromaeosaurs and claim the carcass for itself.

Pachycephalosaurus didn't hesitate a moment longer.
The herd turned away from the river and ran back through
the trees.

The acrid smell of smoke still hung over the forest,
but it seemed that they had circled around the center of the
fire.

The light was fading as the herd reached the rocky
hillside. It had been a strange and anxious day for
Pachycephalosaurus.

He watched as his herd settled themselves for the night,
and then, with a soft sigh, he too slept.

Quetzalcoatlus

Parasaurolophus

Deinosuchus

Corythosaurus

Oviraptor

76 Spinosaurus

Psittacosaurus

Written by Frances Swann
Illustrated by Pam Mara

Pachycephalosaurus

Anatosaurus

Struthiomimus

Scolosaurus

Rutiodon

Psittacosaurus

The sun was already climbing in the sky over the distant purple hills as Psittacosaurus slowly awoke. He was hungry and not well rested, because it had been a strangely disturbing night. Thunder had rolled back and forth across the plain. Disturbed by it, the herd had sought out a higher shelter than usual.

The herd gradually assembled behind the older males. They protected the females and their young by keeping them in the middle. Then they moved off, walking quietly over the forest floor. Above them the yellow katsura and ginko leaves shaded them from the rising sun. The sharp smell of fallen ginko fruit filled Psittacosaurus's nostrils as he tested the air.

In a short time the herd reached a steep bank.
Here they slowed to let the youngsters cross it.
Psittacosaurus looked out over the hardwood forest
and across the plain. Below him he could see the great
delta that fanned out toward the sea. Several birds
soared on thermals above him. On the far side of the
plain he watched a huge herd of dinosaurs obscured by
a dust cloud moving slowly toward the forest edge.

Hungry now, the herd moved quickly toward their favorite feeding grounds. Every so often Psittacosaurus would grasp a passing cycad leaf, crop it with his powerful beak, and chew it as he walked.

Abruptly, the herd stopped. Over the heads of the animals in front of him, Psittacosaurus could see a small group of large Probactrosaurs. They turned to stare at the herd and then lumbered off a few feet to resume feeding. Noisily they raked down branches with their great thumb spikes. Then they settled again onto all fours to chew enormous amounts of foliage.

The herd moved on past them. They knew that despite their size, the Probactrosaurs posed no danger.

At last the herd settled at a quiet feeding ground. Here they could eat in peace. Moving lightly from plant to plant, the herd grasped, chopped, and chewed the luscious green foliage. Palm-like cycads and big bennettitales leaves disappeared as they browsed. Psittacosaurus chewed idly as he watched the youngsters tackling the ferns of the undergrowth.

The heat of the sun was now beginning to penetrate the forest, and every so often, small lizards would dart in and out of view. A slight movement caught Psittacosaurus's eye. Coiled around a branch was a small snake watching him with unblinking eyes. Psittacosaurus moved past it on all fours, heading for some tasty flowering plants he had noticed.

The herd was now well satisified. With the warm sun on his back, Psittacosaurus rested.

Psittacosaurus felt wakeful and unsettled. Still chewing, he moved a little away from his herd. Suddenly, the peace of the forest was shattered by a commotion just yards away from Psittacosaurus. Frozen with fear, he dropped onto all fours among the tall ferns.

In front of him through the leaves, he could see a lone Deinonychus. The great creature was on its hind legs, its huge body towering over a Shamosaurus. The Deinonychus bellowed as the Shamosaurus swung its heavy tail club at the predator's ankles.

Deinonychus lunged repeatedly at the Shamosaurus, but the Shamosaurus was too agile for it. The Shamosaurus swung its tail club again. This time it drew blood, and the Deinonychus turned to escape. Psittacosaurus heard it crashing through the undergrowth as it fled.

When Psittacosaurus finally stood up again, the Shamosaurus had gone and the forest was calm.

Psittacosaurus rejoined his herd when they started to move. The forest seemed secure and safe again as they ambled on, travelling more slowly now in the sultry heat.

All of a sudden, little mammals startled from
the undergrowth ran toward them. The herd, instantly
sensing great danger, rose on their hind legs and ran
panic-stricken, pursued by a large group of
Deinonychus. Headlong they ran, terror driving them
onward, gaining with every yard over their hunters.

Underfoot, decaying branches littered the,
moss-covered ground, and young trees slowed their
progress. Slowly the sounds of pursuit faded behind
them.

Abruptly, the dark shade of the redwood trees gave way to the glare of sun on sand. The herd stood, flanks heaving with exhaustion. On a soft sand bank by the river, Psittacosaurus blinked in the bright light. Shaken by their narrow escape, the herd rested for a while. Keeping close to the edge of the forest, they moved on following the course of the river. Every so often a heron would flap off in front of them or a crocodile would silently slip back into the water. Otherwise all seemed peaceful, and Psittacosaurus began to relax.

Around a bend in the river, the herd came upon three female Bactrosaurs at a nest site. One female was covering her newly laid eggs with sand. The other two moved menacingly toward the herd. Quickly and warily, the herd skirted the nest site.

A sudden thrashing commotion at the river's edge caused the herd to stop and stare. In the churning water Psittacosaurus could see a pair of crocodiles twisting and turning as they tugged at a small dinosaur carcass. Not far from them was a flock of flamingos standing statue-like and unbothered.

The herd moved on, and the ground underfoot became wetter as they reached the edge of a shallow lake. Disturbed by their presence, a couple of basking turtles fell back into the water with a loud plop. In the shallow water Psittacosaurus could make out the darker shadows of darting fish.

A slight sound made Psittacosaurus look up. Across the lake, a group of Segnosaurs splashed toward him through the shallows with their broad feet.

The Segnosaurs posed no threat, and the herd watched them curiously. In the distance Psittacosaurus noticed the vast dark shape of a Pterosaur soaring high above the water.

Slowly the herd turned away from the lake. The air was cooler now. Soon the light would begin to fade. The herd must feed again and find a safe resting place for the night. With a last glance at the lake, Psittacosaurus followed the others back into the shade of the forest. Pleasantly tired, he felt he would sleep well that night.

Quetzalcoatlus

Parasaurolophus

Deinosuchus

Corythosaurus

Oviraptor

Spinosaurus

Rutiodon

Written by David White
Illustrated by Pam Mara

Pachycephalosaurus

Anatosaurus

Struthiomimus

Scolosaurus

Rutiodon

Psittacosaurus

As the sun rose above the horizon of the valley, the creatures of the river bank began to stir. Rutiodon was already awake. She was keeping a constant watch over the nest of eggs she had laid two days earlier. Soon, they would be ready to hatch.

Rutiodon stretched her legs, which were stiff from the cold. She was hungry after the long night. It was now time for her to go to the river to hunt for fish.

She raised herself on her four powerful legs and moved off in the direction of the river. A small Coelurosaur darted out of her path as she made her way through the ferns and horsetails. The Coelurosaur was no match for Rutiodon, who was a powerful creature. She was almost twelve feet long, with many sharp teeth in her long jaws. She was also well armored against attack.

Soon, Rutiodon reached the river. She slid into the clear waters with hardly a sound. She began to swim upstream. Only her eyes and the nostrils just in front of them appeared above the water.

Rutiodon swam swiftly, her great tail sweeping from side to side, propelling her through the water. Her long jaws snapped shut on the fish. There were plenty for her to eat. Other animals, too, were hunting the fish. On the far side of the river, Rutiodon could see a group of Cyclotosaurs in the water. There were enough fish for everyone.

When she had eaten her fill, Rutiodon returned downstream. She clambered up the bank, anxious to return to the place where her eggs were hidden. She did not dare to leave them unguarded for too long. The eggs of a Rutiodon were tempting food for many animals in the river valley.

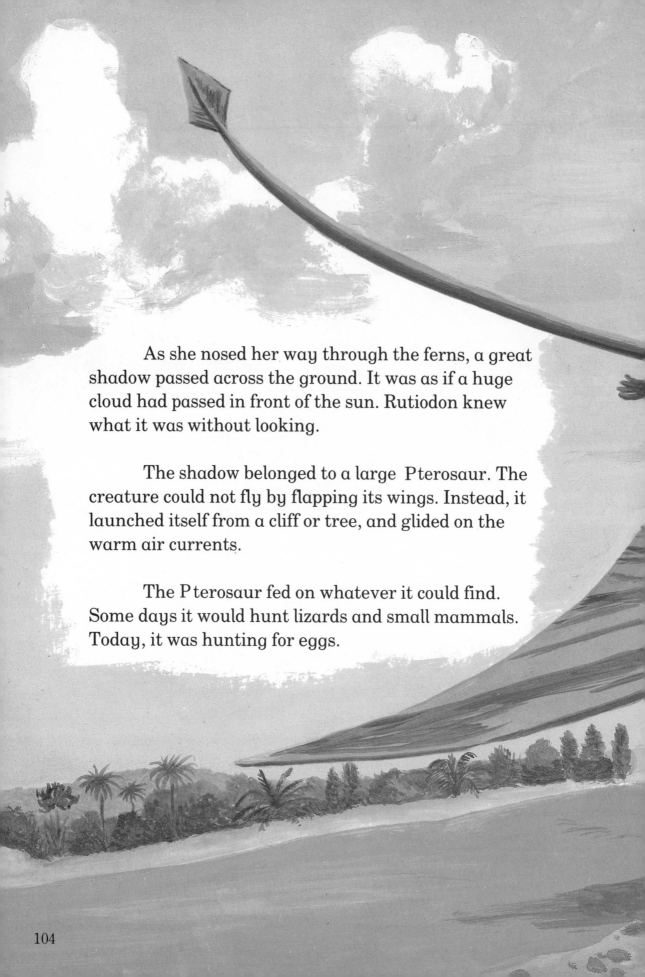

As she nosed her way through the ferns, a great shadow passed across the ground. It was as if a huge cloud had passed in front of the sun. Rutiodon knew what it was without looking.

The shadow belonged to a large Pterosaur. The creature could not fly by flapping its wings. Instead, it launched itself from a cliff or tree, and glided on the warm air currents.

The Pterosaur fed on whatever it could find. Some days it would hunt lizards and small mammals. Today, it was hunting for eggs.

Rutiodon moved quickly to protect her eggs. She covered them with her great body. Hissing through her nostrils, her jaw gaping, she warned off the Pterosaur. The creature swooped once, saw it was useless, and backed away. Then the Pterosaur disappeared to look for easier prey.

The danger had past. Rutiodon could now doze in the midday sun while she digested her meal. Occasionally there were interruptions, and Rutiodon would half open her eyes. She saw Stagonolepis lumbering through the undergrowth. He looked threatening, with big bony plates on his back for protection. Rutiodon knew she need not fear him.

Stagonolepis was not looking for trouble. He was
not interested in the eggs Rutiodon was guarding.
Instead, he grubbed in the ground for the juicy roots of
plants. Eventually he moved away, snuffling as he
went.

The sun was now at its height. The air grew sultry. Away to the northwest, the sky began to darken. The sound of thunder rolled across the valley. Forks of lightning shot down from the upper air. Rutiodon knew instinctively what was to follow. A sudden roaring sound grew louder and louder. A flash flood was coming.

The river, swollen with rain, tumbled down the valley. Muddy water broke over the river banks and swept off anything in its way.

Rutiodon carefully put her eggs in her mouth and carried them to the safety of higher ground. Other animals were not so quick to escape. Henodus, a flat-headed creature encased in a thick shell, was swept off his rock. Mastodonsaurus, who was grazing on the river bank, struggled to stay upright as the torrent swirled around his feet. He, too, was swept downstream.

Suddenly, it was quiet. The flood subsided as quickly as it had risen. The river returned to normal. The only evidence of the flood was a thick carpet of mud spread across both banks.

Rutiodon remained near her eggs. In her new hiding place, away from the river, there were new dangers. Rutiodon could see the edge of the pine woods, where herds of Plateosaurs grazed. Suddenly, there was a sound of breaking foliage. The Plateosaurs paused in their eating, their long necks bending as they turned to see the cause of the noise.

Coelophysis scampered out of the woods, pursued by two Ornithosuchus. Coelophysis dodged this way and that, tiring the mighty pursuers. In the end, the Ornithosuchuses gave up the chase. Instead, they turned on a third Ornithosuchus.

Soon the pine woods echoed with the sound of animals snapping and tearing at each other's flesh. The two Ornithosuchus finally brought down the third. The struggle was over.

However, the danger was not past for Rutiodon. Coelophysis headed straight for her after he had escaped from the Ornithosuchuses. Now he circled around the eggs, snatching and biting with his grasping claws and pointed beak. Rutiodon lunged at him angrily. Coelophysis danced away and then danced back again, looking for a way around Rutiodon.

Finally, the Coelophysis gave up. He was hungry, and he was using up valuable energy. He must find easier prey. As suddenly as he had come, he dashed off into the ferns.

Rutiodon could now relax for a while. Soon it would be night again. New dangers would appear. In the dusk, Rutiodon could again leave the eggs to go down to the river for fish. The river was calm and clear, as if the torrent of the day had never happened. Rutiodon swam lazily, enjoying the cool water. Then she returned to her eggs. For the first time that day, she slept.

Quetzalcoatlus

Parasaurolophus

Deinosuchus

Corythosaurus

Oviraptor

116 Spinosaurus

Scolosaurus

Written by David White
Illustrated by Pam Mara

Pachycephalosaurus

Anatosaurus

Struthiomimus

Scolosaurus

Rutiodon

Psittacosaurus

The rocks of the foothills cast long shadows in the first sunlight. A python, which had slept against a tree stump during the night, uncurled and slithered away. All was still. Then slowly, one of the rocks began to move. It was Scolosaurus. As he lay flat against the ground the heavy armor on his back made him look like a piece of rugged rock.

Scolosaurus liked the safety of hills. If he could not find a cave or rock for shelter, his camouflage would always protect him. He could also walk more safely there than he could in the swampy forests. There was no danger of getting bogged down.

Now he needed food. The grasses of the mountains were sparse and dry. He wanted the green and juicy plants of the woods. He set off for the trees in the valley below.

Scolosaurus knew a glade where the most succulent foliage grew. Here, magnolia and climbing roses flowered. Bees, attracted by the bright colors, carried pollen from one to the other.

Scolosaurus browsed peacefully among the undergrowth. The peace was soon disturbed by the sound of an animal crashing through the foliage.

Struthiomimus burst into the glade. He was a tall creature, with long legs and a long neck. His three-toed feet enabled him to run away quickly from any attacker. Now he needed to use them.

Close after him came Dromaeosaurus. He was far smaller than Struthiomimus, but much more dangerous. This fierce little animal had wickedly sharp claws on his hind legs, which he used to slash at his victims.

Struthiomimus ran around the glade, dodging this way and that. Speed was his only defense against Dromaeosaurus. Scolosaurus took little notice of the chase. With his heavy armor, he was well protected against creatures like Dromaeosaurus. Only his underbelly was vulnerable to attack. This is why he took so much care to protect it.

After circling the glade, Struthiomimus suddenly darted into the trees. Dromaeosaurus did not bother to follow. The chase had tired him. He turned and retraced his steps. There would be other prey for him.

Now the sun was higher, and the forest grew hotter and more humid. Scolosaurus felt thirsty. It was time for him to go down to the river to drink. The river ran through a plain beyond the wood. As Scolosaurus left the shelter of the trees, he was glad he had the protection of his armor.

Across the river plain, Scolosaurus saw herds of Parasaurolophus and Trachodons. Like him, they were going to the river to drink. Most animals visited the river at some time during the day. This made it a dangerous place. The meat-eaters could be sure of a kill if they lay in wait long enough.

Today, there were no signs of the meat-eaters.
Side by side with the Trachodons, Scolosaurus drank
the clear water of the river. The only sound to disturb
the peace was the buzzing of flying insects and the
flutter of dragonflies.

Suddenly, Scolosaurus noticed that the
Trachodons beside him had vanished. He could see the
reason for this reflected in the river. The image of
Gorgosaurus appeared in the water. Scolosaurus
twisted around to face him, just as Gorgosaurus lunged
forward. The huge jaws and savage teeth of the mighty
meat-eater snapped shut close to Scolosaurus's face.

Instinctively, Scolosaurus took up a defensive position. He tucked his great legs under his body and lowered himself to the ground. There was no gap between his armor and the ground. Gorgosaurus circled around him, roaring angrily.

The meat-eater began to lunge at Scolosaurus in an effort to turn him over. This would be the end for Scolosaurus. Quite unprotected and unable to regain his upright position, he would be easy prey for the sharp teeth of Gorgosaurus. He must do everything in his power to prevent it.

Luckily, he was equipped with a heavy tail, and armed with two spikes at the tip. As Gorgosaurus stood astride him, Scolosaurus lashed upward at the meat-eater. Gorgosaurus reeled back, roaring with pain. Gorgosaurus lunged again and the Scolosaurus's tail hit him again just below the throat. Gorgosaurus was almost thrown to the ground.

Finally, Gorgosaurus turned away. He had enough of Scolosaurus and his spiny tail. He moved off down the river bank. This time, it was the Gorgosaurus who was trapped. Facing him was Styracosaurus. With his frill of spikes, he was a fearsome sight. Gorgosaurus hesitated for a moment. If he could get around the side of Styracosaurus, he could deal with him.

Styracosaurus did not give him the chance. With a bellow, he began to charge straight at the meat-eater. The dust flew up behind him as he approached. Gorgosaurus tried to sidestep him, but he was too slow. Styracosaurus landed a stunning blow on his right side.

Gorgosaurus lost his footing and crashed to the ground. Scolosaurus did not wait to see what happened next. Wisely, he took the chance to slip away from the river, across the flood plain toward the woods.

By now it was late afternoon. The shadows had begun to lengthen. The woods looked darker and more threatening. Scolosaurus moved quickly through the undergrowth, as dozens of smaller creatures scampered across his path.

Soon he emerged from the woods, and began the long climb up the foothills to his home. As he climbed, he saw the shape of other animals in the dusk. There was Ankylosaurus, searching for a crevice in the rocks in which to spend the night. Like Scolosaurus, he was safe in the open of the plateaus. He, too, carried heavy armor on his back, and his tail wielded a fearsome club.

Eventually, Scolosaurus reached his resting place. The journey back from the river had been long and he was tired. He sank down, his legs tucked under him. As the sun set and night covered the land, he slept.

Quetzalcoatlus

Parasaurolophus

Deinosuchus

Corythosaurus

Spinosaurus

Oviraptor

136

Spinosaurus

Written by David White
Illustrated by Pam Mara

Pachycephalosaurus

Anatosaurus

Struthiomimus

Scolosaurus

Rutiodon

Psittacosaurus

The dawn arrived suddenly at the edge of the desert. One minute, the plains were cloaked in darkness. The next, they shimmered in the harsh subtropical sun.

Although the sun was above the horizon, the air was still chilly with night. In the shadows cast by a rocky outcrop, Spinosaurus and his mate woke and stirred themselves.

Slowly, Spinosaurus raised himself from the squatting position in which he had slept, until he stood on all four limbs. He knew that he must get warm quickly. Once his blood was warm, he could move fast — faster than the creatures whose blood was still cold.

Spinosaurus emerged from the shadows into the sunlight and looked around him. Then, purposefully, he turned his body until one side was facing the sun. This was so that the sun's rays could heat the blood circulating through the great sail on his back.

Spinosaurus felt the warmth coursing through his veins. His limbs loosened and his brain became more alert. Soon, he was ready to hunt for his prey.

He moved off across the plain, his lowered head swinging from side to side. He was searching for tracks in the sand. Soon he found what he was looking for. There were three pairs of tracks, left by large, three-toed creatures. The hunt was on.

Spinosaurus found his prey on the broad plain of the river. Three Ouranosaurs were feeding on the vegetation that grew near the river. They stood on their broad hind limbs, tearing at the plants which grew in the crevices of the rocks.

Scenting Spinosaurus in the wind, they lowered themselves onto all fours and began to lumber away from the danger. Spinosaurus gave chase.

However, the Ouranosaurs were not easy prey, for they could run as fast as Spinosaurus. This was because their blood, too, had been warmed in the sails on their backs.

Yet Spinosaurus was able to keep up with the Ouranosaurs. He would have caught one of them but they suddenly split up. As each Ouranosaurus ran off in a different direction, Spinosaurus hesitated. Which one should he pursue?

His hesitation allowed the Ouranosauruses to escape. Spinosaurus halted and watched them go. Slowly he returned to the banks of the river. If he could not eat, he could at least drink. He drank warily, watching for the giant crocodiles that inhabited the riverbank. These enormous animals would lie in wait for dinosaurs who came to drink at the river.

Spinosaurus returned to the open plain. In the
distance, he could see a great cloud of dust. This was a
clear signal that a herd of Sauropods was on the move.

As Spinosaurus approached the herd, he could see that it was a large one. Some 20 to 30 Brachiosaurs were making their slow way across the plain. The adults stayed on the outside of the herd, while the young were kept inside. This was to give them protection from attack.

Spinosaurus was interested only in the young Brachiosaurs. However, the adults made a defensive wall with their bodies, so that it was impossible for him to reach them. Spinosaurus angrily snapped and tore at their massive legs, but to no avail.

Finally, he turned away in frustration.
Spinosaurus was tired and dusty and hot. The sun was
now high in the sky. There was no shade on the plain,
so Spinosaurus turned toward the sun, so that the
sun's rays did not strike his sail head-on. When he was
cooler, he continued the hunt. He saw flying reptiles
circling in the distance—a sign that some large
creature had died. As he approached, he saw it was the
carcass of Titanosaurus, a Sauropod.

Several Quetzalcoatluses were perched on the carcass, tearing at the flesh. Spinosaurus chased them away. He was hungry, and he eagerly began to eat. But his meal was interrupted by a roar. Tyrannosaurus, too, had seen the flying reptiles and had come to feed on the carcass. Now it was Spinosaurus's turn to be chased away.

Spinosaurus was no match for Tyrannosaurus. Besides, a fight could damage the precious sail on his back.

Disappointed and still hungry, Spinosaurus returned to the river bank. His arrival surprised Gallimimus, who was foraging for insects and lizards. The hunter lunged at his prey, but Gallimimus was too fast. As Spinosaurus's jaw snapped shut, the creature sprang away, disappearing into the foliage.

Spinosaurus decided to rejoin his mate on the higher ground. Together, they moved across the plain in the heat of the afternoon, ever watchful. Eventually, they found what they were looking for – the undisturbed carcass of a Parrosaurus. The animal had been killed by a Tyrannosaurus when it became separated from the herd. The Tyrannosaurus had eaten its fill, and left the rest to the scavengers of the plain.

Spinosaurus and his mate ate eagerly. This time they could eat as much as they wanted without being disturbed.

As the shadows lengthened, Spinosaurus and his mate returned to the rocky ledge. The evening was cool after the intense heat of the day. Spinosaurus settled down to sleep.

FACTS ABOUT DINOSAURS
Anatosaurus and the Late Cretaceous World

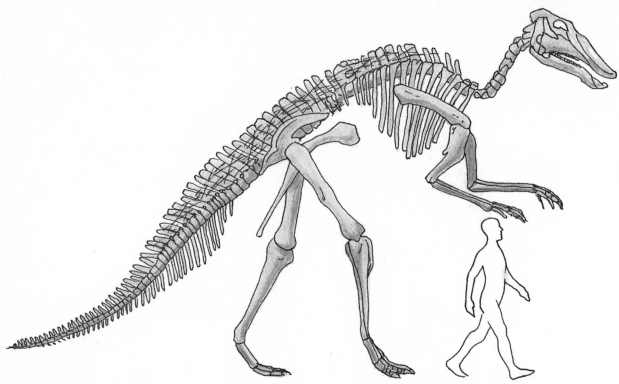

The skeleton of Anatosaurus compared in size with a man

The time of Anatosaurus

The Mesozoic Era, known as the Age of the Dinosaurs, lasted from 225 million years ago to 65 million years ago. Palaeontologists divide this age in to three periods: the Triassic, the Jurassic and the Cretaceous. Anatosaurus lived in the second half of the Cretaceous period, some 70 million years ago. We know this because bones and even pieces of mummified skin have been found in the rocks that were laid down in that period. Anatosaurus lived right up to the end of the Mesozoic Era, until the point when, mysteriously, all dinosaur life on Earth ended.

The land of Anatosaurus

Toward the end of the Age of the Dinosaurs, the world began to look more like it does today. The two supercontinents of Laurasia and Gondwanaland had broken up to form the present continents, which were separated from each other by vast oceans. Dinosaurs were no longer free to roam the world.

Anatosaurus lived in great numbers in North America. The land looked very different then. It was generally flatter. The central range of mountains had not yet been formed. It may also have been intersected by a vast inland sea which extended from the north to the south.

The family tree of Anatosaurus

Anatosaurus was one of the first of the Hadrosaurs, or "duck-billed" dinosaurs. Hadrosaurs were by far the most successful of all the ornithopods living in the Late Cretaceous period. The first Hadrosaur, Batractosaurus, lived in Mongolia 100 million years ago. By 60 million years ago-they had spread to Asia, Europe and North America.

There were three main groups or branches of the Hadrosaurs: the flat-headed Hadrosaurs, the solid-crested Hadrosaurs, and the remarkable hollow-crested Hadrosaurs. (Scientists are not certain what these crests of

156

hollow bone were for, but they think they may have acted as recognition signals). The group that changed least during the 40 million years of their existence were the flat-headed Hadrosaurs, among them Anatosaurus.

Other plant-eaters

Plant-eating Hadrosaurs were the most successful dinosaurs of the Cretaceous period. They completely dominated the North American and Canadian forests, browsing among the trees at the forest's edge. Brachylophosaurus was one of them. Brachylophosaurus had a strong bony face-plate which was probably used in combat with members of the herd. However, Hadrosaurs, like all plant-eaters, were docile creatures, and they would not have used their hardened skulls to fight off predatory meat-eaters.

The meat-eaters

If the Hadrosaurs had been allowed to browse undisturbed, they would have stripped the forests bare. They were prevented from doing so by the meat-eating dinosaurs, the lizard-hipped Carnosaurs, who attained a terrifying power and size during the Cretaceous period. The best known is Tyrannosaurus Rex. This was the largest flesh-eater of all time, almost **45 feet long and weighing 10 tons.** However Deinonychus, a far smaller Carnosaur, was probably more fearsome even than Tyrannosaurus.

Although it was only 6 feet long, it wielded a sickle-shaped claw which enabled it to overcome plant-eaters much longer than itself.

Birds and plants

Much of the bird and plant life of the Cretaceous period would have been recognizable to us today. Besides the older trees, such as conifers and ginkgoes, there were pines, firs, oaks, ash, poplars, maples and sycamores. Among the birds, Graculavus looked much like a present day cormorant and Plegadornis resembled a heron or a stork.

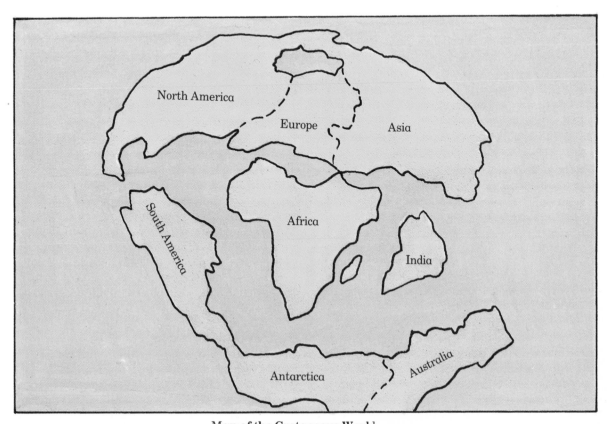

Map of the Cretaceous World

Deinonychus and Early Cretaceous North America

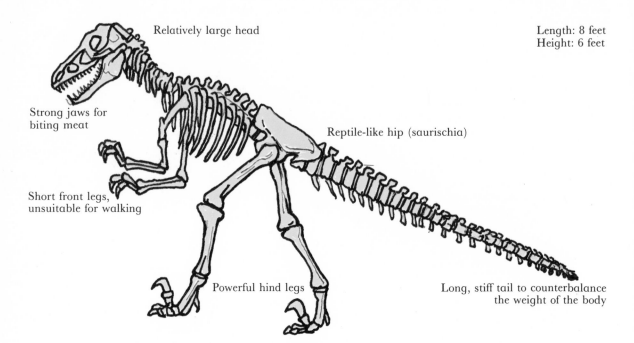

Relatively large head

Length: 8 feet
Height: 6 feet

Strong jaws for biting meat

Reptile-like hip (saurischia)

Short front legs, unsuitable for walking

Powerful hind legs

Long, stiff tail to counterbalance the weight of the body

Skeleton of Deinonychus

When did Deinonychus live?
The Age of the Dinosaurs began about 225 million years ago and lasted for some 180 million years. Scientists have divided this era, which has been called the Mesozoic, into three periods. The first was the Triassic, the second the Jurassic and the third the Cretaceous. Deinonychus lived during the early part of the Cretaceous. It lived about 125 million years ago.

Where did Deinonychus live?
The fossils of Deinonychus have been found in Montana in the United States but Montana was a very different place 125 million years ago. There were no Rocky Mountains. The earth movements that were to result in the Rockies had not even begun. [The landscape was very much like that depicted in the story about Deinonychus and would only become mountainous toward the end of the Cretaceous period.]

It is also interesting to note that western North America was not linked to the eastern part of the continent. It is thought that a shallow sea ran from Canada down to the Gulf of Mexico. Instead, scientists believe, the western part of the continent was linked with Asia. The fact that dinosaurs, similar to Deinonychus have been found in Asia but not in eastern America, seems

to support this idea. Indeed, Deinonychosaurs may have first evolved in eastern Asia.

The Terrible Claw
Deinonychus means 'terrible claw' and it is easy to see why scientists gave it this name. The second toe on each hind foot ended in a 5 inch long claw. There can be little doubt that this was its main killing weapon. Deinonychus could also run very fast. When it saw a likely victim its speed would enable it to run the victim down. When Deinonychus had reached its prey it would leap upon it and kick and slash at it with its claw, just as some birds do.

Some scientists think that Deinonychus may have hidden in ambush for its prey, alternatively it may have hunted in packs as lions do today. It certainly had a larger brain than other dinosaurs and may have been intelligent enough to hunt in groups.

Deinonychus Ancestors
Deinonychus was a meat-eating dinosaur of the Saurischian, (lizard-hipped) group. All the meat-eating and some plant-eating dinosaurs belonged to this group. All plant-eating dinosaurs belonged to the Ornithischian, (bird-hipped) group.

158

Deinonychus clearly represented a distinct form of meat-eating dinosaur. Scientists have therefore placed it and a few similar dinosaurs, in a special family known as Deinonychosaurs. It is thought that this family was an offshoot of the highly successful Coelurosaur family which survived throughout the entire Age of Dinosaurs. The fast-running and agile Deinonychosaurs were certainly very different from the larger and more ponderours Carnosaurs such as Tyrannosaurus rex. They were much more like the small Coelurosaurs which could scamper around in the undergrowth. It is thought that one type of Coelurosaur changed into the Deinonychosaurs at the start of the Cretaceous period, about 135 million years ago. Phaedrolosaurus, a dinosaur from China, may have been one of these ancestral Deinonychosaurs.

A Time of Change
Deinonychus lived during the early part of the Cretaceous period, a time of great change for the dinosaurs. Throughout the previous ninety million years the Saurischian dinosaurs had ruled the world. The future belonged to the Ornithischians.

During the long Jurassic period, the most important type of plant-eater had been the Sauropods. Sauropods were giant Saurischian dinosaurs with long tails and long necks. Brontosaurus was a kind of Sauropod. By the time Deinonychus hunted in North America, Sauropods were becoming rarer. Their place was being taken by many new kinds of Ornithischians.

Tenontosaurus, was one of these. It belonged to the Iguanodontid family of dinosaurs. This family included the famous Iguanodon from Europe which was related to the highly successful duckbilled dinosaurs. Psittacosaurus was also an Ornithischian dinosaur. It was probably the ancestor of the Ceratopsian dinosaurs, a group which included the mighty Triceratops.

Other animals were changing as well. The flying reptiles were changing from the longtailed forms, such as Rhamphorhynchus, to the short-tailed Pterosaurs. Birds had evolved from reptile ancestors and were developing into a wide range of species.

The early Cretaceous period was an important time for life on Earth.

The Deinonychus with (inset) the large sickle-shaped claw on its hind led with which it attacked its prey.

The Skeleton of Pachycephalosaurus Compared in Size with a Man

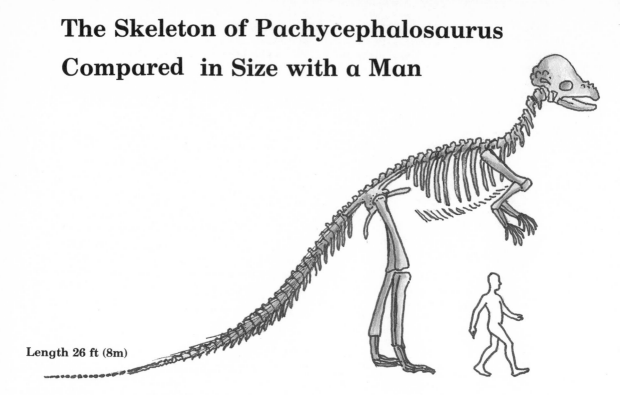

Length 26 ft (8m)

Pachycephalosaurus and the Cretaceous World

The age of the Dinosaurs

The word dinosaur is derived from two Greek words meaning "terrible lizard." All the dinosaurs lived in the Mesozoic era, 225 to 65 million years ago, when the continents were much closer than today. At one time, much of the land was one giant continent called Pangaea. This great mass broke up over many millions of years, and segments drifted apart to become our present continents.

No man has ever seen a dinosaur – man did not appear on earth until a mere 2 to 3 million years ago. So how do we know so much about dinosaurs?

Fossil Finds

Our knowledge comes from fossils, which have been discovered all over the world. Fossil skeletons, eggs, nesting sites, tracks, dung, imprints of skin, and even mummified stomach contents have been found. New finds constantly update our view of the dinosaurs and their world.

When Pachycephalosaurus lived

The Mesozoic Era is divided into three periods— Triassic, Jurassic and the Cretaceous. Pachycephalosaurus lived at the end of the Cretaceous period, which lasted from 135 to 65 million years. The word Cretaceous means chalk. During this time great beds of chalk were formed and the continents took on their present shapes. At the start of the Cretaceous period the weather was mild, but by the end it was quite a lot colder.

The land was low-lying, and it was a time of high sea levels, with many delta, rivers, lakes and swamps. Many new types of plants evolved during the Cretaceous period. Flowering plants appeared for the first time. Many of these plants have survived and would be familiar to us today.

All about Pachycephalosaurus

Pachycephalosaurus belonged to a group of dinosaurs called Pachycephalosaurus, meaning "thick-headed reptiles." At 26 feet (8m) long, Pachycephalosaurus was the largest of a group of thirteen known types. These have been found as widely apart as North America, Asia, England and Madagascar.

Pachycephalosaurus was a herbivore (plant eater) who walked upright on its hind legs. It probably lived in small herds in the drier highland areas, much as goats do today.

Pachycephalosaurus had a high domed skull with a massively thickened skull roof. It is presumed that the males would have defended their territories by having "head-butting" contests. Present day goats and rams behave the same way.

Pachycephalosaurus lived 75 to 64 million years ago. The relationship of Pachycephalosaurus to other groups of dinosaurs is still unclear.

**

Stegosaurus (above), like Pachycephalosaurus, was discovered in North America.

Psittacosaurus and the Cretaceous World

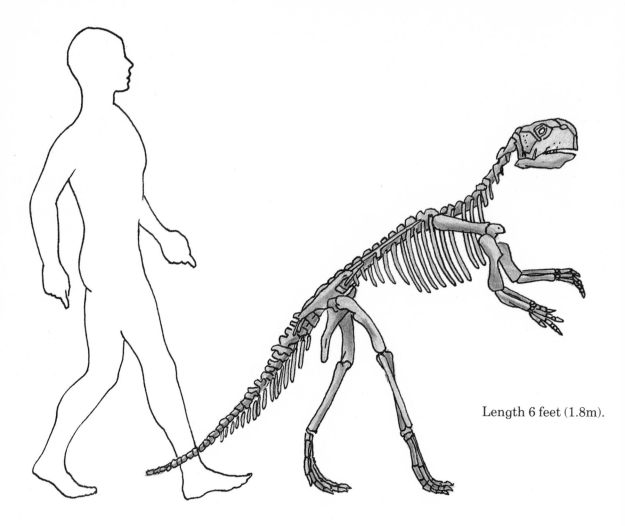

Length 6 feet (1.8m).

The skeleton of Psittacosaurus compared in size with a man

The Age of the Dinosaurs

The word *dinosaur* is derived from two Greek words meaning "terrible lizard." All the dinosaurs lived in the Mesozoic Era, 225 to 65 million years ago, at a time when the continents were much closer to each other than today. At one time much of the land was one giant continent called Pangaea. This great mass broke up over many millions of years—and segments drifted apart to become our present-day continents.

No human being has ever seen a dinosaur. Humans did not even appear on Earth until 2 to 3 million years ago. How then do we know so much about the dinosaurs?

Fossil Finds

Our knowledge has come from fossils that have been discovered all over the world. People have found fossil skeletons, eggs, nesting sites, tracks, dung, imprints of skin, and even mummified stomach contents. Every day new finds change our view of the dinosaurs and their world.

When Psittacosaurus Lived

The Mesozoic Era is divided into three periods: Triassic, Jurassic, and Cretaceous. Psittacosaurus lived in the middle of the Cretaceous period, which lasted from 135 to 65

million years ago. The word *Cretaceous* means
"chalk". During this period, great beds of chalk
were laid down and the continents took on their
present-day shapes. At the start of the
Cretaceous period the weather was mild, but by
the end it was quite a lot colder.

The land was low-lying and it was a
time of high sea levels with many deltas, rivers,
lakes and swamps. Many new types of plants
evolved during the Cretaceous period.
Flowering plants appeared for the first time. By
the end of the Cretaceous period many trees and
plants that are familiar to us today existed.

All About Psittacosaurus

Psittacosaurus lived in Mongolia. He was a
Ceratopsian (horned face) dinosaur. It is
probable he could use his hands both to grasp
foliage and to walk. The long tail was used as a
counterbalance when he ran; he would have
relied on speed to escape predators.

The arrival of many new types of
plants probably caused the evolution of
Psittacosaurus's parrot-like beak, which
enabled him to crop them.

Two of the tiniest dinosaur remains
ever found were skulls of baby Psittacosaurus.
The young would have been 16 inches (40cm)
and 10 inches (25cm) long. They had large eyes,
and their teeth were already worn from eating
plant food.

Psittacosaurus probably laid eggs like
Bractrosaurus, but no one knows how much
parental care they gave their young.

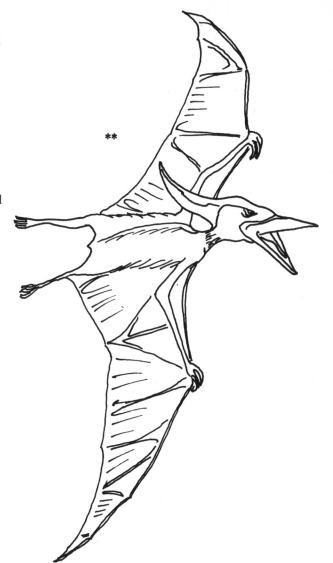

**Psittacosaurus and Pterosaur (above) have similar
parrot-like beaks.**

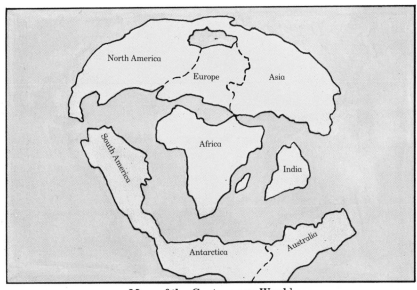

Map of the Cretaceous World

Rutiodon and the Triassic Era

The skeleton of Rutiodon compared in size with a man

The time of Rutiodon

The beginning of the Mesozoic Era was the Triassic Period. It was called Triassic because three rock layers ("tri" means three) dating from this period were found in Germany.

The Triassic Period was between 225 and 193 million years ago.

Rutiodon lived during the Late or Upper Triassic Period; that is, in the second half, some 190 million years ago.

The land of Rutiodon

By the Late Triassic Period, the vast supercontinent Pangaea had split up to form Laurasia to the north and Gondwanaland to the South. Laurasia included modern North America, Europe and Asia. This is where Rutiodon lived.

Rutiodon lived near pools and rivers, just as crocodiles do today.

The family tree of Rutiodon

Rutiodon belonged to the Thecodonts, or "socket-toothed" reptiles. These were very important families since they led to the crocodiles, dinosaurs and Pterosaurs.

The family tree of Rutiodon

Thecodonts evolved 226 million years ago, right at the beginning of the Triassic Period. The first were the Proterosuchians. These were heavy sprawling creatures. They were followed by the Pseudosuchians, which were much lighter and more nimble. Then came the Aetosaurs, the armored plant-eaters, and finally the flesh-eating Phytosaurs.

Rutiodon was a Phytosaur. Fish-eating Phytosaurs dominated rivers and pools until they were replaced by crocodiles. They looked very similar to crocodiles. The only difference was that their nostrils were close to their eyes, while a crocodile's are at the end of its snout.

Other flesh-eaters

During the Triassic Period, two kinds of meat-eaters evolved: large and small. The small meat-eaters were called Coelurosaurs. They made up for their size with their speed. One of the most successful was Coelophysis. This creature was about 10 feet in length, with a long thin tail to balance it when it ran. Its bones were thin and delicate to keep its bodyweight light.

The large meat-eaters were the Carnosaurs. Many scientists think that Ornithosuchus was the first of the Carnosaurs. It was the most fearsome dinosaur of its time. Its only real enemy was another Ornithosuchus.

Among the fish eaters was Cyclotosaurus. As large as a crocodile, Cyclotosaurus had weak legs and needed to stay in water to support its body. It opened its mouth by raising its skull rather than dropping its lower jaw.

Plant-eaters

Plateosaurus was a lizard-hipped dinosaur, almost 20 feet long, that lived in the lowland swamps. It was a Prosauropod and the forerunner of giants like Diplodocus. It shared its environment with numerous amphibians. Among the amphibians, Mastodonsaurus was by far the largest. Its skull alone was over three feet long.

Stagnolepis looked fiercer than it was. It was an Aetorsaur, one of the armor-plated plant-eaters. It had a pig-like nose and weak teeth.

Henodus was a reptile which looked like a turtle. In fact Placodonts like Henodus did eventually evolve into marine turtles.

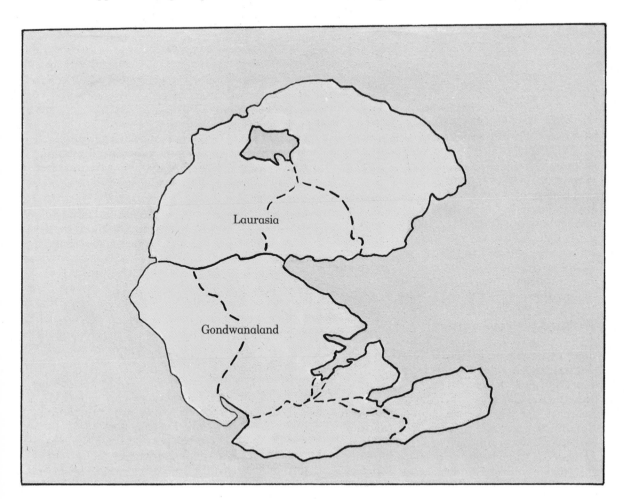

Map of the Triassic period

Scolosaurus and the Cretaceous World

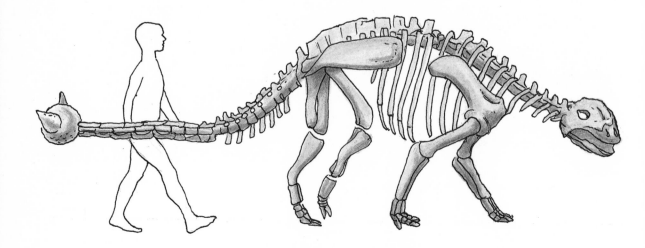

The skeleton of Scolosaurus compared in size with a man

The time of Scolosaurus

Although fossilized remains of Scolosaurus are very rare, there is enough evidence to suggest that Scolosaurus lived at the very end of the age of dinosaurs; that is, in the late Cretaceous period, between 100 million and 65 million years ago. The reason there are so few remains is that Scolosaurus lived in the upland areas, where no sediments were formed. Most of our evidence about dinosaurs comes from sedimentary rocks.

The land of Scolosaurus

The Cretaceous period was a time of immense change. Seas divided the northern supercontinent of Laurasia in two, to form Asiamerica (eastern Asia and western North America) and Euramerica (Europe and eastern North America). The collision of Europe and North and South America, which were joined for the first time, began to push up the present day Rockies and the Andes.

Scientists think that Scolosaurus probably lived at the foot of these new mountain ranges. Scolosaurus must have been a successful dinosaur, since remains have been found throughout the northern hemisphere, in Asia, Europe and North America. No remains have been found in the southern continents of Africa, India, and Australia.

This is because the continents had separated from the northern landmass, so the dinosaurs were no longer able to move from one to the other.

The family tree of Scolosaurus.

Scolosaurus belonged to the family of Ankylosaurs, or "armored dinosaurs." The earliest Ankylosaur was probably Scelidosaurus, who lived in early Jurassic times, 195 million years ago. The family of more than 30 types of Ankylosaurs developed into two distinct branches. On the one side there were the lightweight Ankylosaurs, with narrow heads and without tail weapons. On the other side there were the heavyweight Ankylosaurs, armored like tanks and armed with a spike or club on their tails.

Scolosaurs, an advanced member of the Ankylosaur family, belonged to the armored branch.

Other plant-eaters

Plant-eating dinosaurs dominated the late Cretaceous period. Besides the Ankylosaurs, the other main plant-eaters were the Hadrosaurs and the Ceratopsians. Parasaurolophus, was a striking-looking Hadrosaur, with a hollow crest that measured over six feet from the snout to tip. Trachodon, or Anatosaurus as it is alternately named, was a flat-headed Hadrosaur. Both these creatures were harmless and inoffensive creatures. Their defence lay in flight rather than fight.

Other plant-eaters, however, were not so docile. Ceratopsians were like rhinoceroses, with heavy bodies, sturdy legs and horns on their faces. Some of them, like Styracosaurus, had a frill of spikes round their necks. Their formidable features were enough to drive away any meat-eating dinosaur.

Meat-eaters

Carnivorous dinosaurs had an important function in the late Cretaceous period. By preying on the plant-eating dinosaurs, they prevented the forests from becoming over-browsed. The most impressive meat-eaters were Tyrannosaurus and his cousin, Gorgosaurus. But other, smaller meat-eaters could be equally fearsome. Dromaeosaurus, one of the family of Coelurosaurs, made up for his size with a sickle claw, which he used to attack far larger creatures.

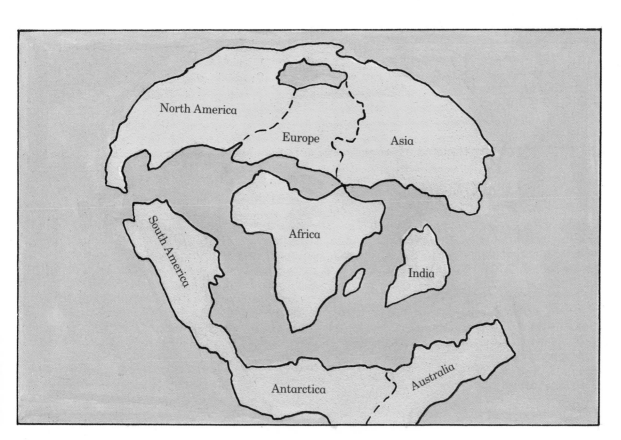

Map of the Cretaceous World

Spinosaurus and the Cretaceous World

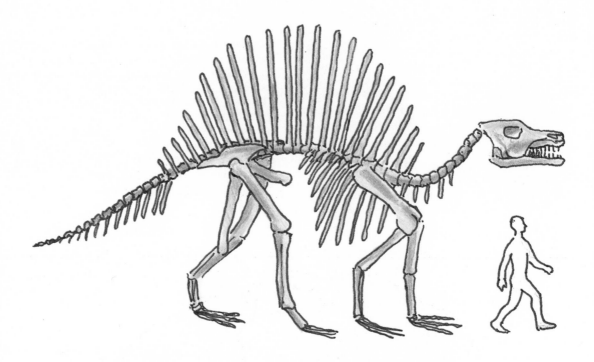

A speculative skeleton of Spinosaurus compared in size to a man.

The time of Spinosaurus

The Mesozoic Era, or the "age of dinosaurs" as it is sometimes known, was between 225 million years ago and 65 million years ago. Geologists divide the era into three periods: the Triassic, the Jurassic and the Cretaceous.

The first two periods are much shorter than the third. The Cretaceous Period lasted for 71 million years. Spinosaurus lived at some time during this period.

The land of Spinosaurus

In the Cretaceous Period, the continents separated and acquired something like the shape they have today. The continent of Africa separated from Europe and Asia.

Spinosaurus lived in North Africa. Fossils have been found in Egypt, which is why Palaeontologists have called it *Spinosaurus aegypticus*. The climate of North Africa was then subtropical and more moist than it is today.

The family tree of Spinosaurus

Spinosaurus belonged to the Carnosaur family. Carnosaurs evolved in the Triassic Period. They soon achieved large sizes. Teratosaurus, who lived 200 million years ago, was 20 feet long. In the Jurassic Period, Carnosaurs like Megalosaurus (the first dinosaur to have been discovered in 1822) and Allosaurus appeared. This branch of the family developed into the fearsome Tyrannosaurus in the Cretaceous Period.

Another branch resulted in Spinosaurus, who is an interesting example of how a Carnosaur adapted to climatic conditions. Most Carnosaurs lived in forests, swamps and jungles. Spinosaurus lived on the edge of the desert. It evolved its sail to cope with the intense heat, just as Dimetrodon did in the Permian Period.

Other meat-eaters

Spinosaurus had many meat-eating

competitors. Chief among them was his Carnosaur cousin, Tyrannosaurus. But there were others like the enormous Quetzalcoatlus. This was a Pterosaur and probably the largest flying creature that ever lived. The creature had a wingspan of 39 feet and weighted more than 180 pounds. It scavenged for food, feeding on the bodies of dead dinosaurs.

Plant-eaters

Once the southern continents, like Africa, had separated from the northern continents, the dinosaurs were no longer free to move throughout the world. This meant that dinosaurs evolved differently in different parts of the world.

In the northern continents, like North America, a new generation of highly successful plant-eaters evolved – the Hadrosaurs, the Ankylosaurs and the Ceratopsians. However, these same types never evolved in the southern continents such as Africa. In these continents, plant-eaters continued to be slow-moving, slow-witted Sauropods like Brachiosaurus and Parrosaurus. They were easy prey for the meat-eaters.

Some plant-eaters did evolve that were able to escape from Carnosaurs. One of these is Ouranosaur.

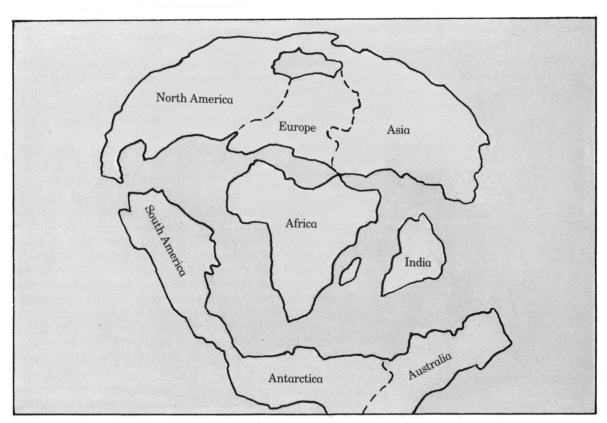

Map of the Cretaceous World

Albertosaurus
(al-BER-tuh-sawr-us)

Albertosaurus was a carnosaur. Carnosaurs were giant flesh eaters with big heads carrying powerful jaws and huge teeth. They had large bodies with powerful back legs and very short front legs. Albertosaurus had slightly longer front legs than *Tyrannosaurus*, a close relative.

Many skeletons of Albertosaurus have been found in the western United States and Canada, and in Mongolia. It is one of the most frequently found kinds of dinosaur fossils. For a long time, scientists thought that certain fossil bones discovered in different places were from separate kinds of dinosaurs. Now, they recognize them all as belonging to the Albertosaurus.

Because Albertosaurus was lighter than *Tyrannosaurus*, it was probably faster. Albertosaurus was about 16 feet tall. It had more teeth than *Tyrannosaurus* and could slash its way into the flesh of its victims, tearing them to pieces before swallowing them.

Length: 26 feet
Weight: 2 tons
Lived: Late Cretaceous
Found: North America

Allosaurus
(Al-uh-sawr-us)

Allosaurus is one of the most fearsome eating machines of the dinosaur age. Remains of these gigantic, flesh-eating dinosaurs have been found in North America, Africa, Australia, and Asia. In one field, scientists found remains of more than 40 Allosaurus.

Allosaurus had a head more than 3 feet long. With jaws hinged like those of a snake, it could swallow its prey whole. Its teeth were curved and up to 4 inches in length. Allosaurus was different from other flesh-eating dinosaurs. It had a ridge along the top of its skull and strange bumps above its eyes. The animal had powerful muscles and a strong tail to give it balance. With only small front legs it had to run and fight on its two powerful back legs. Allosaurus had a single claw 6 inches long on each finger. With these it could slash and tear the flesh of its prey. On each foot were three toes, each with a claw-like talon.

Allosaurus belonged to a family that lived successfully for about 100 million years. It would attack slow, lumbering dinosaurs like *Apatosaurus*. One fossil *Apatosaurus* skeleton has been found with Allosaurus tooth marks on its tail bones.

Length: 36 feet
Weight: 2 tons
Lived: Late Jurassic
Found: North America, Africa, Australia, Asia

Altispinax
(al-tuh-SPY-nax)

This unusual dinosaur lived over 120 million years ago. Fossil bones have been found in England, and it is likely that the animal roamed throughout Europe. Altispinax means "high thorn." Its name comes from the large spines on its back. Each spine was four times longer than the individual back bones it was attached to. A skin probably covered the spines, giving the dinosaur a sail-like fan across its back.

Altispinax was not as big as others in its family. With a length of about 25 feet it was not as big as *Spinosaurus*, which was 40 feet long. All members of this family were flesh eaters. They had sets of small, very sharp teeth. Like other flesh eaters, Altispinax had strong back legs and small, short arms. The sail, or back fin, probably helped the animal cool down in hot climates. Some scientists believe it may have been used to frighten other animals.

Length: 26 feet
Weight: 3 tons
Lived: Early Cretaceous
Found: Northwest Europe

Anatosaurus
(ah-NAT-uh-sawr-us)

One of the last dinosaurs to become extinct, Anatosaurus lived 65 million years ago. Anatosaurus was a duckbill dinosaur and belonged to a family that had jaws shaped like a duck's beak. They were called hadrosaurids and lived for more than 60 million years. Anatosaurus was a typical hadrosaurid. It had up to 1,000 tiny teeth in its mouth for munching vegetation. Many types of Hadrosaurids had a crest, each type shaped differently. Anatosaurus had no crest, but had instead a smooth, rounded head. Anatosaurus had strong back legs and could probably run very fast.

Anatosaurus was built to eat plants, leaves, and small shrubs. One set of remains has been found with pine needles in its stomach, along with seeds and fruit! They could stand erect on their back legs and nibble high branches or rest on their front legs and munch plants. If threatened, they could probably rear up and dash away at great speed. They had strong tails that provided balance when they were running on their back legs. Some Anatosaurus remains have been found with pieces of skin preserved. This is a very unusual find, and scientists have studied the skin carefully. Anatosaurus skin had a pebbly texture, like the skin of a lizard.

Anchiceratops
(ANG-kee-sair-a-tops)

Anchiceratops was on earth for only a few million years, beginning about 69 million years ago. Like all the other dinosaurs, it became extinct 65 million years ago. Anchiceratops belonged to the ceratopsian (horned dinosaur) family and was about 17 feet long. All ceratopsians had a frill made of bone growing from the back of the head. Attached to the frill were very powerful muscles that worked its big jaws. Anchiceratops had a particularly large frill and a massive parrot beak. Three horns grew along the top of its face, two above its eyes and one on its beak.

Anchiceratops roamed the vast plains of Canada during the Cretaceous period, when lush vegetation was plentiful. It liked to crunch tough roots and probably grazed in large herds. They did not eat meat but their tough hides would have protected them well. Only vicious flesh eaters like *Tyrannosaurus Rex* would have been a match for Anchiceratops.

Length: 30 feet
Weight: 3 tons
Lived: Late Cretaceous
Found: Canada

Length: 19 feet, 6 inches
Weight: 7 tons
Lived: Late Cretaceous
Found: Canada

Ankylosaurus
(ang-KILE-uh-sawr-us)

This was the largest, heaviest, and most heavily defended of the ankylosaurid (fused lizard) family to which it belonged. It was more than 32 feet long, weighed 5 tons, and had lots of armor plates over its body. Ankylosaurids were armored dinosaurs with short legs and barrel-shaped bodies. They had short necks and stood low on the ground. Bony slabs, plates, and spikes were set into its skin, under which the flesh grew thick like panels of leather. Dinosaurs of this type had small teeth and jaws with very little muscle power.

Ankylosaurus was one of the most successful of its family at surviving. A great many of them were around at the end of the dinosaur age. They had evolved from earlier types more vulnerable to predators. Several fossil skeletons have been found in Canada, and most seemed to have survived by hiding under their armor. Ankylosaurus had a large bony club at the end of its tail. With this, the dinosaur probably lashed out at flesh eaters, knocking them off their feet or crushing their skulls.

Length: 35 feet
Weight: 1—5 tons
Lived: Late Cretaceous
Found: United States, Canada

Apatosaurus
(ah-PAT-uh-sawr-us)

One of the largest dinosaurs that ever walked the earth, Apatosaurus appeared around 155 million years ago and was a member of the great sauropod (four-legged plant eater) family. All sauropods had stiff limbs and thick legs. Animals like these were slow, lumbering beasts that spent most of their lives eating leaves and large plants. Big animals need a lot of food to satisfy their hunger, and dinosaurs were no exception.

Apatosaurus was once called *Brontosaurus*, or "thunder lizard," because people assume it must have shaken the earth when it walked. After all, it did weigh more than 30 tons. Apatosaurus had a very long neck that stretched more than 20 feet from its shoulder to its head. Scientists used to think the head was small but recent discoveries have shown it to be quite large. It had small teeth shaped like pegs and spent a long time chewing its food. Because these dinosaurs had small brains, scientists used to believe they were stupid. Modern scientists now suspect that they were more intelligent.

Length: 70 feet
Weight: 33 tons
Lived: Late Jurassic
Found: United States (Colorado, Oklahoma, Utah, Wyoming)

173

Archaeopteryx
(ar-kee-OP-ter-ix)

Although many scientists do not consider this a dinosaur at all, others think it was. Its name means "ancient feathers," and it is the earliest known animal to have feathers like a bird. The collarbone and some hip and foot bones, though, are more like dinosaur bones. Archaeopteryx had small muscles and three claws on each foot, with three-clawed fingers half way along each wing. Unlike birds, which have no teeth, this animal had small teeth. It also had scales on its face. From these facts it is possible to show that Archaeopteryx could not have flown very well. It would have fluttered around just above the ground like a frightened chicken.

Archaeopteryx is believed to be the link between land dinosaurs and true birds. For that reason, some scientists claim it is not a dinosaur at all, but the first real bird. It probably got its feathers from scales that split and allowed air to pass through. This would help Archaeopteryx get airborne – but just barely! It was probably descended from *Compsognathus*, which had a long neck, a very long tail, and light bones, just like Archaeopteryx.

Length: 3 feet
Weight: 20 pounds
Lived: Late Jurassic
Found: England, southern West Germany, United States

Bagaceratops
(bah-gah-SAIR-uh-tops)

A ceratopsian (horned dinosaur), this little plant eater was only 3 feet long. He was an earlier member of the family to which *Anchiceratops* belonged. Bagaceratops had a relatively small face with a parrot-like beak. This helped the animal tear up small roots and shrubs to eat. He had no teeth.

Horned dinosaurs are famous for their neck frills made of bone and their several large horns. Bagaceratops had only one small horn just above its beak. It also had a small neck frill and would have been easy prey for flesh-eating dinosaurs. Bagaceratops has been found in Mongolia, and it is not known if they were common throughout the world. Compared to other horned dinosaurs, Bagaceratops looked like a small rhinoceros and may have lived in small groups for survival. Unlike other horned dinosaurs, Bagaceratops could not stand on its back legs.

Length: 3 feet, 3 inches
Weight: 1000 pounds
Lived: Late Cretaceous
Found: Mongolia

Barapasaurus
(bah-RAH-puh-sawr-us)

Barapasaurus means "big leg lizard" and is a combination of Indian and Greek words. It is called Barapasaurus because it had large legs. Unlike most other sauropod (lizard feet) dinosaurs, Barapasaurus did not have thick legs. Its limbs were long and slim, and it had a short head and spoon-shaped teeth. Some scientists believe it should belong in a family of its own. [Most put it among a group of lizard-foot dinosaurs separate from other groups like *Diplodocus* and *Brachiosaurus*.] The most notable difference between Barapasaurus and other sauropods is that it had longer legs, a taller neck, and a comparatively shorter tail. Scientists used to think dinosaurs like these spent all their life in lakes or rivers. They now think Barapasaurus lived by grazing and eating almost continuously. Dinosaurs like Barapasaurus first appeared almost 200 million years ago. They led to large numbers of giant plant eaters found all over the world. Barapasaurus probably died out around 150 million years ago.

Length: 60 feet
Weight: 28 tons
Lived: Early Jurassic
Found: Central India

Brachiosaurus
(BRAK-ee-uh-sawr-us)

This dinosaur has a length of more than 75 feet. It is one of the biggest ever found. The first Brachiosaurus was discovered in 1900 at the Grand River Valley, Colorado. When scientists put its bones together they discovered that its front legs were much longer than its back legs. This is why they called it Brachiosaurus, which means "arm lizard." All other dinosaurs had their longest legs at the back.

Brachiosaurus has a very long neck and a small head with little teeth. Its back is strong and arched with a relatively short tail. Brachiosaurus was very bulky and probably weighed more than 75 tons. It could have looked over the top of a three-story building and probably munched vegetation from tall trees.

Some people used to think Brachiosaurus lived in water, keeping only its long neck above the surface. Scientists now think it roamed around on land. It may have had a long trunk from the two big nostrils on the top of its head. No one knows for sure. Its been 130 million years since Brachiosaurus roamed the earth, and only the bones have survived.

Length: 70–90 feet
Weight: 80–100 tons
Lived: Late Jurassic
Found: United States (Colorado), Algeria, Tanzania

Brachyceratops
(brak-ee-SAIR-uh-tops)

One of the smallest of the short-frilled ceratopsids (horned dinosaurs), Brachyceratops has been named from a group of only five fossils. These were found together in one place in Montana. Each dinosaur was about 6 feet long. Some scientists thought they were not just small ceratopsids. They thought they were baby *Monoclonius* dinosaurs. The bones certainly looked like them and had the same features. Then the fossils of an adult were found, and now most scientists agree that these five examples represent a special type within the family of horned dinosaurs.

Brachyceratops had a very short neck frill made of bone. It was not unlike *Bagaceratops*, although it had two horns above its eyebrows in addition to a large horn on its nose. Brachyceratops lived about 75 million years ago, or 4 million years after Bagaceratops. It may be an early member of the family that led to *Monoclonius* and the giant *Triceratops*. All these were short-frilled dinosaurs.

There were many members of the short-frilled ceratopsian family, including *Centrosaurus, Eoceratops, Monoclonius, Pachyrhinosaurus* and *Styracosaurus*. All had horns, short neck frills made of bone, and scaly skins. Some had holes in their neck frills, while others did not. Some members of the family had bony spikes, and all known members of the family came from North America. Of course, it is always possible that some fossil remains may be found outside this region, but it is unlikely.

Length: 6 feet
Weight: 500 pounds
Lived: Late Cretaceous
Found: United States (Montana), Canada

Brontosaurus. See *Apatosaurus*.

Camarasaurus
(KAM-uh-ruh-sawr-us)

In several ways, Camarasaurus is similar to *Brachiosaurus*, except it is smaller. Like all other dinosaurs (excluding *Brachiosaurus*), its back legs are longer than its front legs. It has nostrils on top of its head, its neck is fairly short, and it has a deep skull and small teeth. The discovery of baby Camarasaurus fossils has helped scientists understand how dinosaurs looked as they grew up. When born they had big heads, short necks, and stubby tails. They changed as they developed.

The brain of Camarasaurus was small compared to its body. Its nose was on top of its head, just in front of its eyes. These dinosaurs must have led a lazy, peaceful life. Their size and tough hide would not make them good prey for flesh eaters, who probably left them alone. Camarasaurus probably wandered through the swamp and forest continually munching. Its little mouth had to feed a very large body.

Length: 60 feet
Weight: 20 tons
Lived: Late Jurassic
Found: United States (Colorado, Oklahoma, Utah, Wyoming)

Camptosaurus
(KAMP-tuh-sawr-us)

This one animal gave its name to an entire family of dinosaurs called "bent lizards" (camptosaurids). They are known to have lived more than 140 million years ago, during the late Jurassic period. Camptosaurids had strong back legs with hooves on their feet. This allowed them to run away from trouble quickly. Camptosaurids are named for their thigh bones, which were bent. They would sometimes stand erect and use their long tongues to pull leaves and foliage from shrubs.

Camptosaurus varied in size from 4 feet to nearly 20 feet. It had a small horned beak with which it could cut leaves and thin branches. Like many other dinosaurs, Camptosaurus could breathe while it chewed. This was possible because the passage that led from its mouth to its stomach was different from the passage that led from its nose to its lungs. Camptosaurus has been found in Europe and North America. It was an ancestor of the family of *Iguanodon*. It was more primitive, however, with four toes on each foot and without a spike on its thumb.

Length: 23 feet
Weight: 1,100 pounds
Lived: Late Jurassic/Early Cretaceous
Found: Western Europe, western North America

Centrosaurus
(SEN-truh-sawr-us)

This dinosaur belonged to the family of short-frilled ceratopsians (horned dinosaurs). Others were the tiny *Brachyceratops* and the much larger *Monoclonius* and *Pachyrhinosaurus*. These were almost as big as Centrosaurus. Like *Monoclonius*, Centrosaurus had a single horn on the top of its nose that curved forward instead of back. It also had a bumpy frill with two pieces of bone shaped like hooks. Centrosaurus had small hooves like a rhinoceros and very thick legs. Each back leg had four stumpy toes and each front foot had five "fingers." Centrosaurus had very strong jaw muscles to help it grind tough food. Scientists believe Centrosaurus traveled in herds. A single fossil find of eighteen separate animals has been discovered in Alberta. The most famous ceratopsian dinosaur is *Triceratops*. They lived mostly in great herds and roamed far and wide for root food and plants. In this way they must have been like great herds of bison ambling across the prairie.

Length: 20 feet
Weight: 2 tons
Lived: Late Cretaceous
Found: Canada (Alberta)

Ceratosaurus
(sair-AT-o-sawr-us)

Ceratosaurus means "horned lizard" and was so named because it belonged to an unusual family of horned flesh eaters. It is thought to have been related to *Allosaurus*, another flesh eater. But Ceratosaurus is the only dinosaur of its kind known to have had a horn on its nose. Ceratosaurus was up to 20 feet long and had a row of small, bony plates running down its back. It had short front legs with four fingers, each with a small claw. Each foot had three toes, also clawed. Ceratosaurus had a large head and a lightweight bone structure. Its teeth were shaped for tearing flesh and killing large animals.

Ceratosaurus probably hunted in packs. Scientists have discovered sets of Ceratosaurus footprints, suggesting that they roamed in groups. It probably lived about the same time as *Megalosaurus* but a long time before *Tyrannosaurus*, another flesheater. Dinosaurs like these would have been feared by all other animals. They were big and powerful and had large appetites.

Length: 20 feet
Weight: 1 ton
Lived: Late Jurassic
Found: United States (Oklahoma, Colorado, Utah), East Africa

Cetiosaurus
(SEET-ee-o-sawr-us)

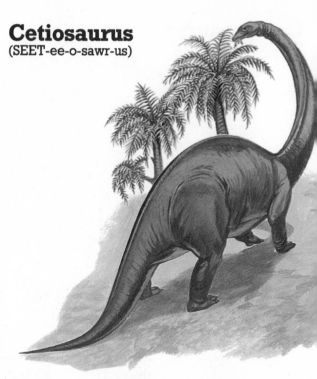

This animal is one of the earliest plant-eating dinosaurs discovered. It probably lived at about the same time *Barapasaurus* roamed the earth. Cetiosaurus belonged to the same group of dinosaurs as *Diplodocus* and probably appeared around 190 million years ago. Scientists can tell that it is an early type, because its bones are not as well developed as other dinosaurs of its family. While others had lightweight back bones, hollowed out to save weight, Cetiosaurus had solid back bones. This observation helps scientists place Cetiosaurus several million years before *Diplodocus*, *Brachiosaurus*, and other types.

Cetiosaurus looked a lot like *Camarasaurus* and had a tail similar to *Diplodocus*. It was smaller than *Camarasaurus* and weighed about 10 tons. Cetiosaurus may have wallowed in rivers and lakes. Scientists are not sure how it lived. They think it probably went down to the water to cool off and wash just like the hippopotamus does today.

Length: 45–60 feet
Weight: 9–12 tons
Lived: Middle to Late Jurassic
Found: Western Europe, North Africa

Chasmosaurus
(KAZ-muh-sawr-us)

Chasmosaurus was a member of the ceratopsian (horned dinosaur) family and similar to *Anchiceratops*. Although smaller than its cousin, Chasmosaurus was a typical horned dinosaur. It had a large neck frill made of bone. Large holes in the bony plate reduced the weight of the neck frill. This made it easier for Chasmosaurus to move its head around. Strong neck muscles were attached to the frill. It needed these to pull out the roots of tough plants. Chasmosaurus had the parrot-like beak of other horned dinosaurs. The frill was longer than the skull itself and covered with skin.

Many Chasmosaurus fossil bones have been found in Alberta. Skin impressions on rock show it had small button-like scales all over its body. With these, its hide was probably quite tough.

Animals like *Tyrannosaurus* would have had a hard time trying to bite through its leathery skin. Their best defense would have been to run away!

Length: 17 feet
Weight: 3—5 tons
Lived: Late Cretaceous
Found: United States (New Mexico), Canada (Alberta)

Coelophysis
(see-lo-FISE-iss)

One of the very first dinosaurs, Coelophysis was known to have lived more than 210 million years ago. In 1947, scientists found more than a hundred skeletons at Ghost Ranch, New Mexico. There were many animals of different ages, and they ranged between 3 feet and 10 feet in length. This discovery has led scientists to believe that they lived in colonies and wandered about in large herds.

Coelophysis was a nimble dinosaur and could probably run very fast. It had slim legs, a long neck and tail and a pointed head with sharp teeth. Feeding on a diet of meat, Coelophysis had three fingers on each hand and a strong muscle joining its hips to its spine. This muscle probably enabled it to twist and turn as it ran, chasing small animals on which it fed.

Some fossil remains of a Coelophysis show babies inside what would have been its stomach. This causes some people to wonder if they were cannibals, eating their young when other food got scarce. Some scientists think they gave birth to live young. Other dinosaurs laid eggs.

Length: 10 feet
Weight: 65 pounds
Lived: Late Triassic
Found: Southwestern West Germany

Coelurus
(see-LURE-us)

Although Coelurus (hollow tail) first appeared around 160 million years ago, it was directly descended from *Coelophysis*. Coelurus was a small, nimble animal about 6 feet long. It had hollow bones for lightness and only three fingers on each hand. The thumb was short but the other two fingers each had a small claw. Coelurus was similar in appearance to *Ornitholestes*, another member of the same family.

Coelurus's head was slightly smaller than a man's hand. In its mouth were rows of small but jagged teeth. These helped it tear small pieces of flesh. Coelurus probably fed on small birds, tiny animals, and dead mammals. With its light weight and strong muscles, it could easily tear through the undergrowth, its head held low, grasping and snatching at wildlife within reach. Some of these small dinosaurs might have fed on the eggs of bigger dinosaurs. They may also have eaten berries or large seeds.

Length: 6 feet, 6 inches
Weight: 30 pounds
Lived: Late Jurassic
Found: United States (Wyoming)

Compsognathus
(komp-so-NAY-thus)

These small, fast running dinosaurs lived at the same time *Coelurus* was known to have been in North America. Compsognathus fossils have been found in Europe. They are among the smallest dinosaurs known. The adults were no more than 2 feet long, about the size of a chicken. They had long necks and very long tails. The stiff tail helped them run very fast and gave them balance. Each hand had two fingers and each finger had a claw. Their legs, twice as long as their arms, had three toes on each foot. Compsognathus means "pretty jaw." Its long, pointed head held two rows of sharp teeth, and it is known to have eaten meat. It had hollow bones, which made it very light. Each animal probably weighed less than 7 pounds. This little dinosaur may have been an egg hunter. There would have been many eggs around in the dinosaur age. Some would have been large enough to provide a juicy meal for these nimble-footed animals.

It is hard to think of this little creature as a real dinosaur, yet he is as much a dinosaur as big *Tyrannosaurus* or giant *Apatosaurus*.

Length: 2 feet
Weight: 7 pounds
Lived: Late Jurassic
Found: Southern West Germany, southeast France

Corythosaurus
(ko-RITH-uh-sawr-us)

Corythosaurus, whose name means "helmet lizard," had a large crest on top of its head. Corythosaurus belonged to the family of duckbill dinosaurs called hadrosaurids. Among other hadrosaurid members were *Bactrosaurus*, *Lambeosaurus* and *Edmontosaurus*. Corythosaurus appeared after *Bactrosaurus* but just before *Edmontosaurus*. It was the only group of duckbills to have a crest on its head. The crest was hollow, narrow, and shaped like a dinner plate. Females and young had smaller crests than males.

Corythosaurus was probably used to feeding on small lizards, insect colonies, and plants. It had a toothless beak with which it would scoop up its food. From fossil remains it seems to have been about 30 feet long and probably weighed around 3 tons. Its big, heavy tail would be useful for keeping it balanced while it stood on its back legs and slowly munched food.

Length: 33 feet
Weight: 2—4 tons
Lived: Late Cretaceous
Found: United States (Montana), Canada (Alberta)

Dacentrurus
(day-sen-TROO-rus)

Belonged to the family of stegosaurid (roof lizard) dinosaurs of which the most famous was *Stegosaurus*. Decentrurus was only 15 feet long, about half the length of *Stegosaurus*, and weighed less than 1 ton. It was one of the earliest stegosaurids. Members of the stegosaurid family were divided into two groups. Some had bony plates down the top of their backs with spines on the tail. The others had mostly spikes and no plates. Dacentrurus had two rows of spikes along its back and tail. Because of its longer legs it stood higher off the ground than some other stegosaurids. Remains of this dinosaur have been found in England. Like other members of the family, it had three toes on each foot and four fingers on each hand. Dacentrurus had a small head and short teeth for eating soft plants. If attacked, stegosaurids would have little defense against meat-eating dinosaurs. They had large fleshy parts and no means of protecting themselves except with their spikes. If attacked, they could lash out with their spiked tail and damage a predator.

Length: 13 feet
Weight: 1,500 pounds
Lived: Middle to Late Jurassic
Found: England

Deinonychus
(dyne-ON-ik-us)

This dinosaur was one of the most efficient hunters of them all. It belonged to the family dromaeosaurid, or "running lizard." Terrifying flesh eaters like *Tyrannosaurus* would tear large dinosaurs to pieces with their huge teeth and massive jaws. Yet they could probably not move very fast. One dinosaur that could was Deinonychus. This dinosaur was the largest in his family, which also included *Dromaeosaurus* and *Velociraptor*.

Deinonychus means "terrible claw." It was given this name because it had a sickle-shaped toe and claw on each foot. The other three toes on each foot were shorter. When running it would lift the claw up and put the outer toes to the ground. The toe with the big claw would be used to rip the bodies of other dinosaurs. Balancing on one leg, it would slash viciously using strong muscles in its thigh. Its tail had long pieces of bone to make it stiff when running. Small arms and hands each had three clawed fingers. Deinonychus had a large head, good eyesight, and sharp teeth.

Length: 10–11 feet
Weight: 250 pounds
Lived: Early Cretaceous
Found: Western United States

Dicraeosaurus
(dye-CREE-uh-sawr-us)

A member of the same family as *Diplodocus*, this smaller relative appeared in the late Jurassic period, more than 150 million years ago. Dicraeosaurus was one of that large group of lumbering plant eaters that lived for more than 100 million years. It was only 40 feet long and stood 10 feet tall. Its name means "forked lizard" and refers to the bones that make up its spine. Some of its back bones are divided to look like a giant Y. The branches on top had large muscles attached to them. Unlike *Diplodocus*, Dicraeosaurus had solid back bones.

This dinosaur weighed about 6 tons and probably spent most of its life peacefully munching plants and lush vegetation. This peace could end, though, if it was attacked by one or more of the fearsome flesh-eaters. It had little or no defense and might have escaped by walking into deep water. Dinosaurs could not swim and would probably not go into rivers and lakes unless attacked. Large, four-footed ones could wade in and escape.

Length: 43–66 feet
Weight: 6–9 tons
Lived: Late Jurassic
Found: Tanzania

Dilophosaurus
(dye-LO-fuh-sawr-us)

This animal belonged to the megalosaurid (great lizard) family that appeared very early in the Jurassic period, around 200 million years ago. It was related to *Megalosaurus*. Dilophosaurus had a large head and two thin bony crests running from the top of its nose to the back of its head. These gave it its name, which means "two-ridged lizard." When first discovered, scientists thought the crest belonged to another animal because it was found some distance away from the skull. Later discoveries proved the crest came from this dinosaur.

Dilophosaurus had five fingers on each hand. The two inner fingers were very small. The outer fingers had long claws like fangs. These would have been used to lash out at victims, easily ripping into flesh. Its powerful jaws would have easily crushed flesh and bone as it sank its huge teeth into the animal's body. On its feet were three clawed toes and a small "big" toe turned backward.

Length: 20 feet
Weight: 1,500 pounds
Lived: Early Jurassic
Found: United States (Arizona)

Diplodocus
(dih-PLOD-uh-kus)

Diplodocus is one of the most famous of the four-legged prehistoric plant eaters. A complete skeleton of Diplodocus was dug up by the famous Scottish-American millionaire, Andrew Carnegie. It was 88 feet long, including a 26-foot neck and a 45-foot tail. The head was quite small and had two rows of peg-like teeth. These were used to pull leaves from tree branches like a comb rakes through hair.

With its long neck, the dinosaur could see over trees and across great distances. This was just as well. It would not have been a fast mover and proved an easy prey to the big flesh-eaters. Diplodocus weighed more than 11 tons. It needed a special skeleton to support that weight. The dinosaur takes its name, which means "double beam," from small bones beneath the backbone. These had a piece that ran forward as well as another piece that ran back – a double-beamed bone. Diplodocus is one of the longest dinosaurs that ever lived. It is not the heaviest. In fact, for its size, Diplodocus was light. Compare Diplodocus with *Apatosaurus*, which weighed 33 tons and yet was nearly 20 feet shorter in length.

Length: 87 feet
Weight: 7—11 tons
Lived: Late Jurassic
Found: United States (Colorado, Montana, Utah, Wyoming)

Dromaeosaurus
(drom-ee-uh-SAWR-us)

One of the dromaeosaurid (running lizard) dinosaurs like *Deinonychus*, but smaller. Fossil remains show it to have been about the size of a man and to have weighed approximately 100 pounds. Its tail was made stiff by rods of bone and helped keep it balanced when running fast. Dromaeosaurus had a large head which contained a big brain. The dinosaur would have been able to balance itself on one leg with the help of its stiff tail while savagely attacking its prey with its clawed toes.

Dromaeosaurus appeared later than its relative, *Deinonychus*, and stalked the earth in the late Cretaceous period, about 70 million years ago. Because Dromaeosaurus was so much smaller it probably had best pickings among the tiny animal life. Many small reptiles and mammals would have been attacked by this fast-moving dinosaur. Dromaeosaurus lived about the same time as *Velociraptor*, although it appeared earlier.

Length: 6 feet
Weight: 100 pounds
Lived: Late Cretaceous
Found: Canada (southern Alberta)

Dromiceiomimus
(dro-miss-ee-o-MY-mus)

This dinosaur belonged to the family of ornitho-mimids (ostrich dinosaurs). They were called this because they looked like ostriches with a long tail and no feathers. Unlike most other dinosaurs, ornithomimids were very fast. Nothing could catch them. At full speed, Dromiceiomimis was quicker than a galloping horse. It had a long slender neck and a large head. Although about 12 feet long, its thin, light bones gave it a weight of only 220 pounds. Its neck was long and slender, supporting a large head with a big brain and huge eyes. They had no teeth, but each foot had three toes. Each hand had three spindly fingers, each with a tiny claw.

Dromiceiomimus means "emu mimic." It was named this because it looked like an emu. The dinosaur was in the same family as *Ornithomimus* and *Struthiomimus*. Unless surprised while feeding, it is unlikely that the Dromiceiomimus was easy prey. It probably fed on seeds, small eggs,

insects, or other pickings in woods and on plains. If disturbed, it would lift up its stiff tail, raise its head, and run quickly to safety. Dromiceiomimus lived at the end of the great age of dinosaurs. Members of the ornitho-mimid family spanned 100 million years, from the mid-Jurassic to the end of the Cretaceous period. Most ornithomimids lived during the middle to late Cretaceous period. They repre-sent the end of a long line or ostrich dinosaurs that began with the coelophysids in the late Triassic. The most famous coelophysid was *Coelophysis*, which weighed less than one-third the weight of Dromiceiomimus.

Length: 11 feet, 6 inches
Weight: 220 pounds
Lived: Late Cretaceous
Found: Canada (southern Alberta)

Dryosaurus
(DRY-o-sawr-us)

A member of the large group of "bird-footed" dinosaurs, this one belonged to a family known as the gazelles of prehistoric animal life. They were all small and quite fast, with five-fingered hands and four toes on each foot. They chewed plant food and vegetation with small teeth inside horny beaks. These were very successful survivors. The families in this group lived for more than 100 million years. They were among the first "bird-footed" dinosaurs to appear and lived among types like *Camptosaurus*.

Dryosaurus, which means "oak lizard," was the biggest of the group. Some were up to 14 feet long. A nearly complete Dryosaurus skeleton was found in Utah. From this scientists have discovered it had long, agile legs, which gave it speed when in a chase. It had little else to defend itself with. It would probably forage among vegetation and plant life, always bobbing its head up to watch for big preying flesh eaters!

Length: 9–14 feet
Weight: 120–180 pounds
Lived: Middle to Late Jurassic
Found: Eastern England, Romania, Tanzania, United States (Utah)

Dryptosaurus
(DRIP-tuh-sawr-us)

This animal is one of the most mysterious dinosaurs, because nobody has been able to build up a full skeleton. At least 12 fossil specimens have been found, however. The best skeleton was dug up by a famous dinosaur collector in 1866. He called the dinosaur Laelaps. Because somebody had already given that name to an insect it was changed to Dryptosaurus, which means "tearing lizard." This was an appropriate name. Dryptosaurus was a large meat eater like *Tyrannosaurus*. It was about 25 feet long with curved teeth and three large claws on each foot.

Some scientists think this dinosaur may have been a different member of the *Tyrannosaurus* family. Others think it was closely related to *Megalosaurus*. A few have even linked it with *Iguanodon*! The picture shows how Dryptosaurus might have looked when he roamed the earth around 70 million years ago.

Length: 25 feet
Weight: 1 ton
Lived: Late Cretaceous
Found: United States (New Jersey, Maryland, Colorado, Montana, Wyoming)

Edmontosaurus
(ed-MON-tuh-sawr-us)

This dinosaur was one of the giants in the large family of duckbill dinosaurs. It was as long as 43 feet and could weigh more than 3 tons. It belonged to the group of "bird-foot" families and appeared during the late Cretaceous period, about 72 million years ago. Edmontosaurus were plentiful: they were known to have lived all over the earth.

Edmontosaurus did not have a bony crest on top of its head, as other duckbills did. Its skull was low in front and high at the back. It fed on plants that needed to be chopped up before being swallowed. To do that it had about a thousand teeth in its soft mouth. Scientists know quite a bit about this dinosaur because they have found so many skeletons.

Some scientists think Edmontosaurus had flaps of skin on each side of its nose. When it blew these up like balloons, they made a loud bellowing sound. Like many other animals, dinosaurs probably used these loud noises to communicate.

Length: 33–42 feet
Weight: 2–3 tons
Lived: Late Cretaceous
Found: United States (New Jersey, Montana) Canada (Alberta)

Elaphrosaurus
(eh-LOFF-ruh-sawr-us)

One of the earliest ornithomimids (ostrich dinosaurs), Elaphrosaurus was a relative of *Dromiceiomimus*, *Gallimimus*, *Ornithomimus*, and *Struthiomimus*. It was probably one of the earliest members of that family and fossil bones have been found that date back to the late Jurassic period. Most "ostrich dinosaurs" are found from the Cretaceous period. A distant relative is *Ornitholestes*, a small dinosaur only half the size of Elaphrosaurus.

With long, slender legs and a stiff tail, Elaphrosaurus would have easily sprinted from danger. It had keen eyes and a quick brain. Its diet probably depended on where it lived. Near the sea it might have grubbed around for shellfish or shoveled sand for tiny creatures. Some lived far inland and others foraged among woods and forests. Since it had no teeth, Elaphrosaurus could not have eaten meat.

Length: 11 feet, 6 inches
Weight: 220 pounds
Lived: Late Jurassic
Found: Algeria, Tanzania, Morocco, Tunisia, Egypt, Niger

Eoceratops
(EE-o-sair-uh-tops)

This medium-sized dinosaur belonged to the large family of ceratopsian (horned dinosaurs). The most famous and largest member of this family was *Triceratops*. With a length of about 20 feet, Eoceratops was much smaller than *Triceratops*. Horned dinosaurs varied in size and had different types of horns. Some, like *Brachyceratops*, were no larger than 6 feet and had only one small horn. These appeared around 75 million years ago. *Triceratops* was huge and had three big horns, two of which were 4 feet or longer. *Triceratops* appeared about 67 million years ago. Eoceratops was an early horned dinosaur. It is thought to date back almost as far as *Brachyceratops* and is best known from fossil bones dug up in Alberta. Three small horns on its face crowned a 3-foot-long skull. A short bony neck frill protected the back of its head from the fangs of meat-eating dinosaurs. Eoceratops means "early horned face." It was probably the earliest of its family type.

Length: 20 feet
Weight: 2—5 tons
Lived: Late Cretaceous
Found: Canada (Alberta)

Erlikosaurus
(er-LIK-uh-sawr-us)

Euhelopus
(you-heh-LO-pus)

One of the big plant-eating dinosaurs similar to *Camarasaurus*, Euhelopus, or "good marsh foot," had a longer neck and nose. Like *Camarasaurus*, it had strong teeth that grew around its jaws. Other dinosaurs of this type had teeth growing only in front. Euhelopus had large nostrils on top of its head. Because of this, some scientists think it had a long trunk. That would have made it look very strange. Both *Camarasaurus* and Euhelopus were camarsaurid (chambered lizard) dinosaurs, with hollow chambers in the backbone.

Euhelopus was a little slimmer than *Camarasaurus*, but large members of the family may have weighed as much as 24 tons. The biggest could have been up to 50 feet in length – without trunk. In this picture, Euhelopus is shown without a trunk. From fossil remains, scientists believed they were at home in marshy land at the bank of muddy rivers or in swamps. They would have been safer there than on dry or wooded land where the big flesh eaters roamed.

This flesh eater was found among remains dug up in Mongolia. It belonged to a strange branch of the big carnosaur (flesh lizard) group. Other families belonged to types like *Tyrannosaurus*, *Allosaurus*, and *Megalosaurus*. Erlikosaurus belonged to the family of "slow lizard," or segnosaurid, dinosaurs. It was named in 1980, and most scientists think it was a direct descendent of *Megalosaurus*. Erlikosaurus appeared late, more than 100 million years after *Megalosaurus* first walked the earth.

Erlikosaurus did not look like *Megalosaurus*, though. It looked more like *Deinonychus* in size, but had longer arms and smaller teeth. Its top lip ended in a toothless beak. It had four toes, each with a long claw. It is believed its feet may have been webbed like a duck's. Other members of the same family were even bigger than Erlikosaurus. One, called *Segnosaurus*, was 30 feet long and stood more than 8 feet tall.

Length: 13 feet
Weight: 280 pounds
Lived: Late Cretaceous
Found: Mongolia

Length: 33–50 feet
Weight: 18–24 tons
Lived: Early Cretaceous
Found: China (Shantung)

Euoplocephalus
(you-op-luh-SEF-uh-lus)

Named for its "well armored head," Euoplocephalus was a member of the family of ankylosaurs. These "fused lizards" were best known by the bones of *Ankylosaurus*, the biggest of them all. There were at least twelve different types within the family and Euoplocephalus was typical in size and weight. It probably weighed nearly 3 tons and has been dug up in places as far apart as Alberta and Sinkiang, which is in northwest China.

All ankylosaurs were about the size of a modern battle tank. They had different arrangements of armored bands down their backs with ridged plates and blunt spikes. Euoplocephalus had round nostrils and a horny, toothless beak. Row upon row of armored back plates helped protect it from predators. At the end of its tail it had a large, bony club. Ankylosaurids were among the last dinosaurs to appear before all dinosaurs

became extinct 65 million years ago. Euoplocephalus was well adapted to munching plants and lush greenery while protected from attack.

Two closely related families of ankylosaurs were the "fused lizards" and the "node lizards." Both appeared from a common ancestor at the beginning of the Cretaceous period and have been found all over Europe, North America, and Asia. Node lizards included *Acanthopholis*, *Hylaeosaurus*, *Nodosaurus*, *Panoplosaurus*, and *Silvisaurus*.

Length: 23 feet
Weight: 3 tons
Lived: Late Cretaceous
Found: Canada (Alberta), China (Sinkiang)

Fabrosaurus
(FAB-ruh-sawr-us)

Fabrosaurids, or "Fabre's lizards" were among the earliest dinosaurs known. They were small, the largest as tall as a man, and light-boned. Fabrosaurus was only 3 feet long and had hollow limb bones with small arms and long legs. Each hand had five fingers and each foot had four toes. In its relatively small mouth were two rows of ridged teeth. With these, it could grind small roots and shoots. Fabrosaurus had a broad jaw with holes for new teeth to replace old ones.

Fabrosaurus was closely related to *Lesothosaurus* and *Scutellosaurus*. It appeared late in the Triassic period, more than 200 million years ago. Dinosaurs of the fabrosaurid family lived for at least 70 million years and were like the grazing animals of today. They would have been the gazelles and deer of the dinosaur world. From this line of ancient animals came *Heterodontosaurus, Hypsilophodon, Camptosaurus, Iguanodon, Hadrosaurus, Bactrosaurus*, and many other duckbills, boneheads, and other groups.

Length: 3 feet, 4 inches
Weight: 40 pounds
Lived: Late Triassic/Early Jurassic
Found: South Africa (Lesotho)

Gallimimus
(gall-ih-MY-mus)

With a long neck, bony tail, and strong legs for running, Gallimimus was the largest of the ostrich dinosaurs (ornithomimids). Its name means "fowl mimick" because it seemed to copy the behavior and appearance of certain fowls we know today, like the ostrich and the turkey. With a length of 13 feet, it could probably move quickly on its long legs. Other relatives were *Dromiceiomimus* and *Elaphrosaurus*. Gallimimus had poorly developed hands. They would not have been much use for grasping tiny lizards or tearing open insect nests. Each member of the family of ostrich dinosaurs differed in some way from its relative. Gallimimus had an unusually long snout with a broad, flat end.

Like other members of the family, Gallimimus would quickly sprint away from danger. With long loping legs, it would have looked like an ostrich as it ran. It may have snapped and pecked at dinosaur eggs. Dinosaur eggs were small with thin shells similar to chicken or turkey eggs. A good strong peck from Gallimimus' beak would have been enough to break them open.

Length: 13 feet
Weight: 250 pounds
Lived: Late Cretaceous
Found: Southern Mongolia

Geranosaurus
(jer-AN-uh-sawr-us)

This tiny dinosaur was a close relative of *Heterodontosaurus*, Geranosaurus was among the very first dinosaurs that appeared. They were ancestors of "bird-footed dinosaurs," such as *Fabrosaurus*. Scientists believe they eventually led to the great families of the bonehead dinosaurs like *Pachycephalosaurus*. More than 130 million years before the bonehead dinosaurs, however, the little Geranosaurus roamed large areas of South America and South Africa. At that time, the two countries were joined together. Since then, over millions of years, South America and Africa drifted apart.

Geranosaurus means "crane-lizard." It had tusks as well as teeth that were used for grinding food. Perhaps only males had tusks. Geranosaurus had small tusks in the lower jaw but no sockets for them in the upper jaw. It is believed these little dinosaurs died out around 200 million years ago. Heterodontosaurids did not lead to other, more developed descendents. Yet they came from a line that also produced the "bird-foot" dinosaurs, and scientists think they may still find remains of later members of the heterodontosaurid family. It would not be surprising if they turned up in South America.

Length: 4 feet
Weight: 50 pounds
Lived: Late Triassic/Early Jurassic
Found: South Africa

195

Hadrosaurus
(HAD-ruh-sawr-us)

This was the first dinosaur from North America to be named. Its bones were dug up in New Jersey, and in 1858 it was given a name that means "different foot." This became the family name for a large group of hadrosaurids. The family also included *Edmontosaurus*, which was much bigger and heavier than Hadrosaurus. All duckbills had flat heads with solid bone crests or humps on top. The shape and size of these features varied among different members of the family. Hadrosaurus had a deep, narrow face. It had two rounded humps, one above each eye socket.

Scientists have discovered fossil remains of Hadrosaurus that date back 78 million years, making Hadrosaurus older than *Edmontosaurus*. In fact, they were not very closely related. Both came from an unknown ancestor believed to have been on earth more than 80 million years ago. Some scientists, however, think both types were much older than this. They have found fossil footprints 120 million years old that look just like those made by Hadrosaurus.

Length: 26—32 feet
Weight: 1—5 tons
Lived: Late Cretaceous
Found: United States (New Jersey, New Mexico), Canada (Alberta)

Herrerasaurus
(her-RAY-rah-sawr-us)

This fearsome meat eater belonged to the group of prosauropod ("before the lizard feet") dinosaurs. Prosauropods go back to the beginning of dinosaur life, 220 million years ago. From these different families came the great and gigantic plant eaters like *Cetiosaurus*, *Brachiosaurus*, *Camarasaurus*, and *Diplodocus*. Herrerasaurus was not the earliest prosauropod, but it was the biggest of its family. Its big head had two rows of teeth shaped like sickles. With long back legs and large front legs, it was probably able to move quickly across rough ground. Its front legs probably helped it climb across rocky land.

From bones dug up in Argentina, Herrerasaurus is known to have been about 10 feet long and to have weighed around 220 pounds. Others in the family have been found in China. Not many are believed to have existed. They did not seem to survive beyond the early Jurassic period, about 200 million years ago.

Length: 10 feet
Weight: 220 pounds
Lived: Late Triassic
Found: Northwest Argentina

Heterodontosaurus
(het-er-uh-DON-tuh-sawr-us)

A close relative of *Geranosaurus*, Heterodontosaurus was more advanced and larger. These small dinosaurs would have been on earth at the same time as *Herrerasaurus* and *Fabrosaurus*. All three kinds date back to the late Triassic, more than 190 million years ago. Heterodontosaurus remains have been found in South Africa, Argentina, and China. This animal had one thing in common with people: three different types of teeth. It had sharp, cutting teeth at the front, fangs at the front of the lower jaw, and molars in the back for grinding.

Heterodontosaurus had three toes on each foot and a claw at the back of its heel. It had five fingers on each hand. Like most other members of this family, Heterodontosaurus was small, about 4 feet long. Some of these dinosaurs had muscles in their cheeks. They probably had a mixed diet of small insects and plant roots, with seeds, nuts, and primitive forms of fruit. Heterodontosaurus had small, grasping hands that could forage and grub around for juicy food. There were no defensive weapons on its body. Only the speed of its legs would help it escape attack.

Length: 4 feet
Weight: 50 pounds
Lived: Late Triassic/Early Jurassic
Found: South Africa

Homalocephale
(ho-mah-luh-SEF-uh-lee)

Its name means "level head" because it had a flat top to its skull. There were several bumps on the top of its head and a pattern of small pits. Most remains come from Mongolia and it was probably about 10 feet long. Homalocephale was one of the large family of "bone-head" dinosaurs that lived about 70 million years ago. They are thought to have descended from the family of *Heterodontosaurus* dinosaurs, which lived more than 110 million years earlier. Homalocephale was closely related to *Pachycephalosaurus*.

Like other members of its family, Homalocephale had a very thick skull. This may have been used to attack others that tried to invade its territory, or it may have been used to play. Animals of today often butt heads in play. Homalocephale probably lived on high slopes and on the sides of mountains. Most of its fossil remains have been washed down from high places by fast-flowing streams. These animals walked on their back legs, using their tails as props when standing.

Length: 10 feet
Weight: 200 pounds
Lived: Late Cretaceous
Found: Mongolia

Hylaeosaurus
(hy-LAY-ee-uh-sawr-us)

This primitive ankylosaur ("armored dinosaur") was closely related to *Acanthopholis*. It lived about 120 million years ago and belonged to the "node lizard" group of ankylosaurs. The other group, called "fused lizards," included *Ankylosaurus*. Hylaeosaurus means "woodland lizard," and it was discovered in southeast England as long ago as 1833. It probably had spikes along the sides of its body and plates jutting up along the tail. Underneath, it had a heavily armored back from its head to its tail.

Unlike the "fused lizard" ankylosaurs, Hylaeosaurus and its relatives did not have a thick, bony tail club. Instead of hitting the attacking predator, it may have stood higher on its legs to run away at the pace of a trotting horse. Hylaeosaurus had weak jaws and small teeth. It would spend its time eating ground plants and large insects. Dinosaurs of the ankylosaur families account for one in ten of all dinosaur remains.

Length: 20 feet
Weight: 2—5 tons
Lived: Early Cretaceous
Found: England

Hypselosaurus
(HIP-sih-luh-sawr-us)

This is one of the lesser known members of the sauropod ("lizard foot") dinosaurs within the family of titanosaurids, or "giant lizards" and was a distant relative of the big plant eaters like *Diplodocus* and *Apatosaurus*. The members of the "giant lizard" family each had a steep, sloping head set on a short neck. Their teeth were peg-shaped and their mouths were small. These dinosaurs also had long, slim tails. Hypselosaurus means "high ridge lizard," and this dinosaur was called so because it had a particularly high back. At 40 feet long, it was a relatively small member of the family. Other members of the family were up to 70 feet long.

Scientists have discovered eggs from Hypselosaurus that may be the biggest of all dinosaur eggs. Each egg is 12 inches long and 10 inches in diameter. It could contain almost 6 pints of liquid. The surface of each egg is rough and pitted. Clusters of five eggs have been found in nests. They are the only eggs positively known to come from a specific dinosaur.

Length: 40 feet
Weight: 30–40 tons
Lived: Late Cretaceous
Found: France, Spain

Hypsilophodon
(hip-sih-LO-fuh-don)

This particular dinosaur survived for more than 100 million years. It first appeared at the end of the early Jurassic period and lived until all the dinosaurs died out 65 million years ago. Hypsilophodon belonged to the same family as *Dryosaurus*. It was smaller, perhaps only half the size of its larger relative. These were among the most fleet-footed dinosaurs ever. They could run fast and keep their balance at great speeds. They had horny beaks, and most had small upper teeth. Each foot had three toes and their small hands had five fingers.

Hypsilophodon had a special set of self-sharpening teeth in its cheeks. It may have had two rows of bony studs down the length of its back, and some of the studs may have continued onto the tail. Various skeletons show Hypsilophodon to have been between 4 feet, 6 inches and 7 feet, 6 inches long. Specimens have been found in England and Portugal as well as South Dakota. At least 20 partial skeletons have been unearthed.

Length: 6 feet, 7 inches
Weight: 130 pounds
Lived: Early Cretaceous
Found: United States (South Dakota), England, Portugal

Iguanodon
(ig-WAN-oh-don)

Named "iguana tooth" because it had teeth like modern iguana lizards, Iguanodon is one of the most famous dinosaurs. It belongs to a family similar to *Camptosaurus* but larger, heavier, and better equipped to eat. Its mouth was large, with teeth in the cheeks. In front was a bony beak like *Hypsilophodon*. Iguanodon usually stood on all fours. It had big, strong thighs and three-toed feet. Its smaller front legs each had four fingers and a spiked thumb. When it reared up to rest on the base of its tail, it would have stretched up to 16 feet tall. It had a length of almost 30 feet.

Iguanodon first appeared more than 120 million years ago and lived 55 million years, becoming extinct at the same time as all the other dinosaurs. Other members of the Iguanodon family included *Muttaburrasaurus* and *Ouranosaurus*. Iguanodon probably roamed swampy countryside, wading through hot marshland looking for food. It could wrap its long tongue around reeds and thick grasses. Sucked into its large mouth, small branches and tough roots would be crunched with its two rows of cheek teeth.

Length: 29 feet
Weight: 5 tons
Lived: Early Cretaceous
Found: Europe, Romania, North America, North Africa, Mongolia

Ingenia
(in-JEN-ee-ah)

Oviraptorids, or "egg thieves," was a family with two members. One was called Ingenia, which means "genius." The other, which gave its name to the family, was called *Oviraptor*. Both belonged to a very large group of separate, closely linked families. The group members were called coelurosaurs, or "hollow tailed-lizards," because they all had thin, fragile bones, long legs, and shorter arms. Other important families included *Avimimus*, *Compsognathus*, *Ornithomimus*, *Dromaeosaurus*, and *Stenonychosaurus*. In all, 60 different types of dinosaurs in 14 families made up this group.

Ingenia was discovered in 1981 and had thicker fingers than *Oviraptor*. Of three fingers on each hand, the first was longest, followed by the second. Each finger had a curved claw. At about 6 feet long, Ingenia was a little smaller than *Oviraptor*. It was found in southwest Mongolia, and it is likely that others lived elsewhere in Asia.

Length: 6 feet
Weight: 60 pounds
Lived: Late Cretaceous
Found: Mongolia

Kentrosaurus
(KEN-truh-sawr-us)

One of the stegosaurid, or "plated dinosaur," family, Kentrosaurus means "pointed lizard." It was named for the spines on its back. Other members of this family included *Dacentrurus*, *Stegosaurus*, and *Tuojiangosaurus*. All these dinosaurs walked on four legs and had very tough skins. Kentrosaurus had pairs of short, triangular shaped plates on its neck and shoulders. Halfway along its back, the plates were replaced with long spikes. The spikes were set in pairs along the back and the tail. An extra spike grew from the top of each thigh.

Plated dinosaurs changed from their first appearance in the middle of the Jurassic period 160 million years ago. Various members of the family appeared at different times. Kentrosaurus was known to exist as far back as the late Jurassic, about 150 million years ago. Compared with giants like *Stegosaurus*, Kentrosaurus was quite small. It was little more than half the size of its larger relative.

Length: 17 feet
Weight: 1 ton
Lived: Late Jurassic
Found: Tanzania

Kritosaurus
(KRIT-uh-sawr-us)

Some scientists think this dinosaur was a very close relative of *Hadrosaurus*. It had a flat, broad head and a humped nose. It belonged to the duckbill family and lived toward the end of the dinosaur age. Kritosaurus means "noble lizard." Its humped nose reminded some people of the nose of a noble Roman senator!

Remains of Kritosaurus have been dug up in New Mexico and Baja California. Skeletons show it to have been about 30 feet long and up to 15 feet tall. It probably weighed nearly 3 tons. Duckbill dinosaurs had webbed feet and could probably swim. They would only do this to escape predators. Most of them lived in forests and woods.

Female Kritosaurus laid eggs in nests and stayed to look after them. Most male dinosaurs roamed away from the nest while females nursed the eggs until they hatched. Then they tended the young until they had grown up.

Length: 30 feet
Weight: 3 tons
Lived: Late Cretaceous
Found: United States (New Mexico), Mexico (Baja California)

Labocania
(lab-o-KAY-nee-uh)

A relative of *Tyrannosaurus* and *Megalosaurus*, this Cretaceous dinosaur was a fearsome flesh eater. It was much smaller than *Tyrannosaurus* and has not yet been attached to a known dinosaur family. It probably belonged to a group of more than 15 similar dinosaurs. Labocania had a much bigger head than *Tyrannosaurus* and a much bigger body. In many other ways it was very similar to its bigger relative. With enormous teeth and sharp claws on its toes, Labocania would have been a frightening predator. Yet its weight, which averaged about 3 tons, probably slowed it down and allowed it to be attacked by other flesh eaters. Some scientists think it had a very thick skin, which would have made it tough to kill. Only a few bones of Labocania have ever been found. They were dug up in the La Bocana Roja rock formations in Baja California.

Length: 25 feet
Weight: 3 tons
Lived: Late Cretaceous
Found: Mexico (Baja California)

Lambeosaurus
(LAM-be-uh-sawr-us)

A member of the duckbill family, Lambeosaurus was named after Lawrence Lambe, a Canadian scientist who spent much of his life studying dinosaurs. Literally the word means "Lambe's lizard." There were two types of duckbills. One group had head crests made of hollow bone, and the other group did not. Lambeosaurus was a member of the crested group and was the largest crested type known. Remains have been found in western North America, from Canada to Baja California.

With a very large tail and an enormous crest, Lambeosaurus was a monster, almost four stories tall on his back legs. Some skulls have been found with a crest bigger than the head. Others look like they might have had a small neck frill made of bone. One type had a very deep tail, which would have made it a good swimmer. This would be unusual, since it is not thought dinosaurs were happy in water. Rock impressions of its pebbly skin show Lambeosaurus to have had a leathery hide. Lambeosaurus is known to have lived about 85 million years ago.

Length: 49 feet
Weight: 2—5 tons
Lived: Late Cretaceous
Found: Mexico (Baja California), United States (Montana), Canada (Alberta)

Lesothosaurus
(leh-SOTH-uh-sawr-us)

Named after Lesotho, the country in Africa where it was first discovered, Lesothosaurus was a very close relative of *Fabrosaurus*. It was a member of the "bird-footed" (ornithopod) family. Built for browsing and running away if attacked, the back legs were strong and had three main claws on each foot. In addition, each foot had a small claw higher up the shin. Each tiny hand had four main fingers and a tiny, stub-like thumb. Like *Fabrosaurus*, Lesothosaurus was only 3 feet long and lived in the late Triassic, more than 200 million years ago. Unlike its close relative, it had narrower teeth. Its front teeth were smooth and pointed. Some scientists say the cheek teeth look like serrated arrow heads.

Small dinosaurs of this family are thought by some to have been the ancestors of almost all the "bird-foot" dinosaurs. No larger than a big dog, they survived at least 70 million years before dying out. Eventually, long before they vanished, other more powerful "bird-hips" had arrived.

Length: 3 feet, 4 inches
Weight: 40 pounds
Lived: Late Triassic/Early Jurassic
Found: South Africa

Lexovisaurus
(lex-OH-vuh-sawr-us)

This dinosaur is one of the oldest relatives of *Stegosaurus* known to have been found anywhere. It was very similar to *Kentrosaurus* but lived several million years earlier. It was discovered in remains found around the town of Lyon in France. An ancient Gallic people called Lexovi once lived in the area. Because of this, scientists called it Lexovisaurus ("Lexovi lizard"). Other bones were found in other parts of France, and fossil remains were also discovered in England. Those found in England are for an animal about the same size as *Kentrosaurus*. Some scientists think they have found more remains that suggest some members of the same family were much larger.

With more varied plates and spikes than *Kentrosaurus*, Lexovisaurus had narrow plates on its back and spines on its tail. Like its descendent, it had large spikes protecting each thigh. It is likely that dinosaurs of this type roamed across large areas of the earth. Several members of the same family would cross the same paths many times. More than 4,000 miles separate England from Tanzania, where *Kentrosaurus* was found!

Scientists are not sure why Lexovisaurus, and other members of its family, had bony plates along its back. Some people think it was for protection, although the animal would have been exposed along the sides of its body. Others believe it helped the animal radiate heat and keep its body temperature comfortable.

Length: 17 feet
Weight: 1 ton
Lived: Mid Jurassic
Found: England, France

Lufengosaurus
(loo-FEN-guh-sawr-us)

Distantly related to *Anchisaurus*, but larger, heavier, and stronger, Lufengosaurus belonged to the "flat lizard" (plateosaurid) family. It is known to have appeared about 210 million years ago. This member of the plateosaurid family was found in Lu-feng, making it the oldest dinosaur from China. It had strong jaws and short, widely spaced teeth. Because of this, scientists think it ate small animals as well as munching plants and small trees. Lufengosaurus probably walked on all fours. To get food they could rear up on their hind legs, using their long, strong tails for balance.

For a while, Lufengosaurus and its family relatives may have dominated large parts of the earth. It was the time when dinosaurs were just beginning to appear. Another famous relative, which gave its name to the entire family, is *Plateosaurus*. Different family members have been dug up in North America, Europe, and Africa. They are not thought to have lived long. They probably died out by the early Jurassic period.

Length: 20 feet
Weight: 1,800 pounds
Lived: Late Triassic/Early Jurassic
Found: China

Maiasaura
(mah-ee-ah-SAWR-uh)

Maiasaura is called "good mother lizard" because it was found with nests and babies. It belonged to the group of duckbill dinosaurs. Other members of the same family were *Edmontosaurus* and *Hadrosaurus*. They had flat heads without crests and a long, straight bottom jaw. They would browse among trees and long grasses munching food as they slowly ambled along. Maiasaura was dug up in Montana and had a bony spike growing from the top of its head. This dinosaur was discovered in 1978. With it were several nests, each one 7 feet across and more than 2 feet deep. Each nest was in the form of a mound. The eggs, shaped like sausages, were set out in the mound like spokes in a wheel. Each layer of eggs was separated with a layer of sand. The top layer was completely covered over. The young were found near the nest. This suggests that when they hatched they stayed close to home. These newly hatched Maiasaura were about 18 inches long and had badly worn teeth. The mother probably brought them food.

Length: 30 feet
Weight: 1—2 tons
Lived: Late Cretaceous
Found: United States (Montana)

Mamenchisaurus
(mah-MEN-chee-sawr-us)

This unusual dinosaur was a close relative of *Diplodocus* and *Apatosaurus*. Dinosaurs in this family were unusually long. Mamenchisaurus was discovered in south-central China and named from the area in which it was found – Mamenchi. From its bones, scientists guess that it was about 72 feet long, with the longest neck of any dinosaur yet discovered. In fact, its neck was so long it contained 19 neck bones, called vertebrae. From its "shoulders" to its head, Mamenchisaurus measured 33 feet!

Some of the vertebrae had struts to help stiffen the neck. Some scientists believe it may have developed this neck to reach very high branches of tall trees. Others believe it spent most of its life in rivers and ponds, sweeping its neck around to feed from the bank. This is not very likely. It probably combed leaves from twigs on trees. It may even have reared up to rest on the base of its spine. If it did, it could have reached leaves 50 feet above the ground.

Length: 72 feet
Weight: 10 tons
Lived: Late Jurassic
Found: China (Mamenchi)

Massospondylus
(mass-o-SPON-dih-lus)

Massospondylus was a close relative of *Lufengosaurus* and *Plateosaurus*, and a distant relative of *Thecodontosaurus*, and its name means "bulky spine bone." In most aspects it was similar to its close relatives, except that it was smaller. Dinosaurs of this type were common over 200 million years ago, during the late Triassic and early Jurassic periods. Fossil remains of Massospondylus were found in southern Africa. Bones similar to this type have also been found as far away as India.

Massospondylus had much larger hands than any of its relatives. In each thumb was a large, curved claw. This may have been a defensive weapon, but it is more likely that the claw was used to increase its diet. Instead of munching plants and small animals, it could dig up juicy roots and tear out small trees. This dinosaur had stones and pebbles in its stomach to grind up food. Its primitive teeth were not capable of tearing up plant food in its mouth.

Length: 13 feet
Weight: 1,200 pounds
Lived: Late Triassic/Early Jurassic
Found: South Africa

207

Megalosaurus
(MEG-uh-lo-sawr-us)

This was the very first dinosaur to be named. It was identified in 1824 and called "big lizard" because it was so large. At that time people thought it was just another old reptile. They did not know it belonged to a completely different group of animals that lived many millions of years ago. Described by Oxford University Professor Robert Plot in 1677, the thigh bone of Megalosaurus was said to come from a giant man! Nearly 150 years later it was identified as belonging to a relative of *Allosaurus*. Megalosaurus belonged to a family of at least 17 different types of flesh-eating dinosaurs.

It was a big, heavy predator distantly related to that terrifying meat eater, *Tyrannosaurus*. Megalosaurus had curved teeth with a saw-tooth edge and strong claws on each toe and finger. By studying footprints of this beast found all over Europe, South America, Africa, and Asia, scientists guess that it waddled like a duck, its tail thrashing from side to side as it stumbled along. This is because its toes pointed inward.

Length: 30 feet
Weight: 1 ton
Lived: Early Jurassic to Early Cretaceous
Found: Europe, South America, Africa, Asia

Melanorosaurus
(mel-AN-or-uh-sawr-us)

Dinosaur hunters are unsure about Melanorosaurus. Some think it is the same animal as Euskelosaurus. Others identify it as very similar but different. Whatever it is called, it was a member of the "flat lizard" family named after *Plateosaurus*. These dinosaurs had broad hands and feet. Their legs probably stuck out sideways and they walked on all fours. Some, such as *Lufengosaurus*, could stand upright on their back legs. They all had blunt teeth and chewed plants and possibly small animals.

Melanorosaurus was the longest of the early dinosaurs and had legs like an elephant. Its bones were solid, like those of most dinosaurs of this period. Later, more advanced dinosaurs developed hollow bones to reduce their weight. This gave them greater agility. It allowed them to run and escape danger. They probably survived longer this way. With lighter bones came a better method of moving blood around the body.

Consequently, advanced dinosaurs were able to shed body heat as they ran. Long before that, though, Melanorosaurus was an important early dinosaur.

Scientists have thought a lot about how Melanosaurus and other similar dinosaurs moved around. Some think they were able to trot or run fast to escape danger. Others believe they were more like reptiles, unable to run fast and shed extra heat. Melanosaurus was certainly well developed, and although it appeared early in the age of dinosaurs it was more advanced than some that appeared later.

Length: 40 feet
Weight: 2 tons
Lived: Late Triassic/Early Jurassic
Found: South Africa

Microceratops
(my-kro-SAIR-uh-tops)

Literally named "little horned face," this tiny plant eater is one of the smallest dinosaurs yet discovered. Fully grown, an adult would stretch little more than 2 feet long from beak to tail. It belonged to the family headed by *Protoceratops*. Its other well-known relative was *Bagaceratops*. These were small, primitive, horned dinosaurs. Each had a differently shaped horn or bump on its face. Microceratops had a short neck frill made of bone. A horny beak helped it grovel among the undergrowth for food and a place to hide. Being so small, it would have made easy pickings for meat eaters.

Fossil bones found in Mongolia and east China show that Microceratops had longer back legs than its relatives. These legs were slender and strong enough to support its weight. Microceratops probably foraged on all fours. It would rear up and run on its back legs when startled. This little dinosaur was not around long and soon died out.

Length: 2 feet, 6 inches
Weight: 25 pounds
Lived: Late Cretaceous
Found: Mongolia

Microvenator
(my-kro-ven-AY-tor)

Microvenator is one of the smallest "hollow-tailed lizards" (coelurosaurs) discovered. Its name means "small hunter." This turkey-sized hunting dinosaur was dug up in Montana and lived in the early Cretaceous period. Its hollow bones made it lightweight. Microvenator stood only 30 inches tall, although its total length was almost 4 feet. It had a long neck with a small head. On its short arms were three fingers. Its long tail was built to help the dinosaur balance itself when standing up on its back legs.

Microvenator was related to *Coelurus*, *Ornitholestes*, and *Ornithomimoides*. These fast-moving, pecking little predators existed on earth for several million years. As a group, these families of dinosaurs survived for about 100 million years. All of them were descendents of the late Triassic *Coelophysis*. Although none could fly, they were the equal of pecking birds today. They would have cleaned up food left by larger animals.

Length: 2 feet, 6 inches
Weight: 14 pounds
Lived: Early Cretaceous
Found: United States (Montana), Tibet

Monoclonius
(mon-uh-CLO-nee-us)

This animal is one of the earliest horned dinosaurs to be discovered in western North America. It was called Monoclonius ("single stem") because it had a single horn on its nose and was a member of the family of horned dinosaurs called ceratopsians. There were two types of horned dinosaurs. One type, like Monoclonius, had short neck frills made of bone. The other type had longer frills. Other members of the short-frill type included *Brachyceratops*, *Centrosaurus*, *Pachyrhinosaurus*, and *Styrachosaurus*. The most famous relative was *Triceratops*, the biggest and the most feared.

Some people think *Brachyceratops* was a baby Monoclonius. *Brachyceratops* was about two-thirds the size of Monoclonius. Monoclonius was little more than half the size of *Triceratops*. Its head was large, about 6 feet long, and a single horn grew from the top of its nose. A small bump grew above each eye. The back edge of the neck frill had a row of bony knobs and two spikes that pointed forward. Monoclonius may have used its horn to topple small palm trees and its parrot-like beak to forage for juicy roots.

Length: 18 feet
Weight: 1–8 tons
Lived: Late Cretaceous
Found: Western North America

Muttaburrasaurus
(mut-tah-BUR-rah-sawr-us)

This large relative of *Iguanodon* was named after the place in Australia, called Muttaburra, where it was discovered. First named in 1981, it is one of the few dinosaurs to come from that country. Muttaburrasaurus has a close link with the *Camptosaurus* family. Many of its bones look more like *Camptosaurus* than *Iguanodon*. Because of that, some dinosaur scientists classify it with the *Camptosaurus* rather than the *Iguanodon* family. The differences between the two families are slight. Along with many others, they are all part of the "bird-foot" group called ornithopods. Muttaburrasaurus had a low head with a broad skull. Its mouth swept gently upward and it had teeth like garden shears. These sharp teeth would have helped it eat meat, although no one knows exactly what it did feed on. Like several dinosaurs, it probably ate meat as well as plants and roots. It had a spiked thumb on each hand, like *Iguanodon*, to help it forage or fend off attackers. Members of the *Iguanodon* family appeared at the beginning of the Cretaceous period, about 125 million years ago. Muttaburrasaurus dates from about 105 million years ago.

Length: 23 feet
Weight: 4 tons
Lived: Mid-Late Cretaceous
Found: Australia (Muttaburra)

Nemegtosaurus
(NEH-meh-tuh-sawr-us)

Skull bones found indicate that this dinosaur was a late member of the *Diplodocus* family. It has been named after Mongolia's Nemegt Basin where it was found. *Diplodocus* is not found in rocks from the late Cretaceous. The skull named Nemegtosaurus is very similar to a *Diplodocus* skull. It has the same sloping shape. Other Nemegtosaurus bones have also been found. It may be that *Diplodocus* lived in this later period also, but that no bones have yet been found in rocks that date from this time. Nemegtosaurus was probably as long as *Diplodocus*, with a slender body, long neck, and long tail.
Nemegtosaurus is related to *Mamenchisaurus*. It does not, however, have that dinosaur's extremely long neck. Other members of the family came from the late Jurassic, about 50 million years before Nemegtosaurus roamed these hidden places deep in Asia. It is possible that isolated groups of dinosaurs lived on for millions of years after their relatives had died out. The headless skeleton of another dinosaur was found with Nemegtosaurus. Some scientists believe it was part of the same animal.

Length: 87 feet
Weight: 12 tons
Lived: Late Cretaceous
Found: Mongolia (Nemegt Basin)

Nodosaurus
(no-doe-SAWR-us)

This medium-sized armored dinosaur has been found all over North America, from New Jersey to Wyoming. It had rows of large and small plates down its back and its sides, or flanks. Its skin had bony buttons, called nodes, between its ribs. Small spikes were attached to the plates. It would have been a tough beast to eat! None of these bony plates and spikes were attached to its skeleton. For this reason, dinosaur scientists are not exactly sure where they were positioned.

In some families of armored dinosaurs, each member had a bony club at the end of its tail. Nodosaurus belonged to a group that had no club. Instead, its tail just trailed along the ground as its low head foraged for food. Node dinosaurs have been found in many countries, including France, Spain, England, India, China, and Australia. The largest members of the family were about 25 feet long and weighed more than 3 tons.

Length: 18 feet
Weight: 2—3 tons
Lived: Late Cretaceous
Found: United States (Kansas, Wyoming, New Jersey)

Opisthocoelicaudia
(o-piss-tho-SEE-luh-caw-dee-uh)

When Polish scientists were looking for dinosaurs in the Gobi Desert of Mongolia, they found remains of this animal without its neck bones or a skull. They called it the "backward hollow-tail dinosaur." It had four legs of almost equal length, and its tail was held high. Rigid bone links kept the tail level but about 5 feet off the ground. When they looked further, the scientists found a skull that they called *Nemegtosaurus*. Some experts think the two are the same animal. Others say the head does not match the skeleton found several miles away.

Opisthocoelicaudia may have sat back on the base of its tail. With its front legs and neck up in the air it could have reached very high trees and branches to feed off leaves. Scientists say the bones of this dinosaur are similar to the bones of freshwater turtles. Some turtles prop themselves up on the base of their tails. Some turtles curl their tails round big stones to anchor themselves. The dinosaur may have done this also.

Length: 40 feet
Weight: 15 tons
Lived: Late Cretaceous
Found: Mongolia (Gobi Desert)

Ornitholestes
(or-nith-o-LESS-teez)

A lightly built meat eater, Ornitholestes was called "bird robber" because it was believed to chase primitive bird life. Scientists used to think it was the same as *Coelurus*, but they now see it as a different member of the same family. It had long and slim back legs with short front legs, or arms. With tough feet and a tiny claw on each of three toes, they were fast-running dinosaurs. Capable of dashing through undergrowth and across grassland, they may have preyed on the dead flesh of other dinosaurs. In this way they may have been the jackals of the dinosaur age, tearing up the flesh of dinosaurs killed by the great meat eaters like *Tyrannosaurus*.

With small hands, each supporting three fingers, they probably lived by rummaging and foraging. An almost complete skeleton of Ornitholestes was found in Wyoming. From this, scientists have pieced together a lot of information about the tiny predator. Lizards, frogs, and small mammals would have been easy prey for this fierce little hunter.

Length: 6 feet, 6 inches
Weight: 30 pounds
Lived: Late Jurassic
Found: United States (Wyoming)

Ornithomimus
(or-nith-uh-MY-mus)

Found widely in North America and Mongolia, this dinosaur was called "bird imitator" because it looked like an ostrich without feathers. As a member of the same family as *Dromiceiomimus*, *Elaphrosaurus*, *Gallimimus*, and *Struthiomimus*, Ornithomimus was lightly built with a delicate bone structure. It was basically all neck and tail, held together by a short, plump body. All members of this family had keen eyesight, were quick, and could leap about at great speed. Ornithomimus had a long mouth with no teeth and a small head. It had a large brain and was not stupid. There were three toes on each foot and three fingers on each hand. Its arms were so small they were useless for real work and would have been good only for scratching the ground for things to eat. Feeding off insects, eggs, seeds, and small grubs, Ornithomimus would have little means of defending itself if attacked. This kept it alert for danger. With a top speed of around 35 MPH, Ornithomimus could outpace any other animal.

Length: 11 feet, 6 inches
Weight: 220 pounds
Lived: Late Cretaceous
Found: Western North America, Tibet

Othnielia
(oth-NEEL-ee-ah)

The bones of Othnielia were originally called Nanosaurus. They were discovered in 1877 by the fossil hunter Othniel Charles Marsh. Exactly one hundred years later they were renamed after the man who discovered them. The dinosaur was a small member of the "bird-foot" family named after *Hypsilophodon*. It was much older than others in the same family, such as *Parkosaurus*. Othnielia was very like *Hypsilophodon*, except it had hardened enamel on both sides of its teeth. Its jaws were built to chop plants and chew them up before swallowing. The tip of the pointed mouth had a small beak-like pincer. Its jaws had strong muscles to cope with tough food. It also had an unusual hinge in the back of its mouth. When its upper and lower jaws came together, they swiveled around so both sets of teeth met exactly together.

Like others in the family, Othnielia had three toes on each foot and fingers on each hand. These dinosaurs were among some of the most successful at surviving. They lived about 100 million years before they died out.

Length: 4 feet, 6 inches
Weight: 50 pounds
Lived: Late Jurassic
Found: Western North America

Ouranosaurus
(our-AHN-uh-sawr-us)

One of the strangest dinosaurs, Ouranosaurus was discovered from remains found in West Africa. It belonged to the family of *Iguanodons* and was close in size to *Muttaburrasaurus*. It was a typical duckbill, with a flat head and an upturned mouth. It would often drop down on all fours but could also stand up on its back legs. Members of the *Iguanodon* family have been found all over the world. They stayed on earth for a long time, and Ouranosaurus may have been an ancestor of the duck-billed dinosaurs that appeared in the late Cretaceous period.

One other feature set Ouranosaurus apart from its relatives. It had a thin sail made of skin running from the back of its neck to the end of its tail. There may also have been a piece of skin under its chin. The skin probably carried blood vessels. These would remove heat from the body of the dinosaur. The heat would be carried to the surface of the skin and radiated away into the air. In this way the dinosaur would cool itself in hot weather. In cold conditions, the sail would have gathered heat from the sun. The blood would have carried heat to the body, arms, and legs to warm them.

Length: 23 feet
Weight: 4 tons
Lived: Early Cretaceous
Found: West Africa

Pachycephalosaurus
(pak-ee-SEF-uh-lo-sawr-us)

This dinosaur was a very large member of the "bonehead" family. All members of the family had thick skulls. Some had a thick knob on top of the skull that looked like a crash helmet. Some of these animals were quite small, less than 3 feet in size. A relative, *Homalocephale*, was 10 feet long. Pachycephalosaurus was the biggest of the boneheads and towered above its relatives. It also had the thickest skull, with which it could charge its enemies and knock them senseless. There was only one problem with a thick skull. It left little room for brains!

Scientists have carefully measured the skull of different boneheads and found that Pachycephalosaurus had a dense cap of bone 10 inches thick. It had some small, bony spikes jutting up from its nose and sharp knobs around the back of its head. Charging at full speed, it would have made a terrific impact. It may also have used its head to ram others in its family. Some animals do this today to claim territory or to warn off others. Pachycephalosaurus lived in North America, but others in the large family have been found all over the world.

Length: 15 feet
Weight: 450 pounds
Lived: Late Cretaceous
Found: Western North America

Pachyrhinosaurus
(PAK-ee-rye-no-sawr-us)

Bone hunters in Alberta dug up the fossil remains of a very unusual member of the "horned dinosaur" family. The most familiar member of this family was *Triceratops*. Others included *Centrosaurus*, *Eoceratops*, *Monoclonius*, and *Styracosaurus*. Each had one or more horns on its face. Pachyrhinosaurus had no horn but had a squat stump on the top of its nose. The stump, shaped like a plate, was 22 inches long and 14 inches wide. The bone was 5 inches deep with a volcano-shaped crater in the middle. Bone knobs had grown above the eyes.

All horned dinosaurs had either a short frill or a large frill. Pachyrhinosaurus belonged to the short-frilled family. It had short spikes of bone growing from the back of the frill. Like all horned dinosaurs, it had a parrot-like beak with which it groveled for food. The stump on the nose of this dinosaur might have been used to ram other animals or to knock small trees down by charging them with its head.

Length: 18 feet
Weight: 1—2 tons
Lived: Late Cretaceous
Found: Canada (Alberta)

Palaeoscincus
(pay-lee-o-SKINK-us)

Known only by a single tooth and some odd bones found in Montana, this dinosaur is a member of the "node lizard" family. Some scientists have said it is the same as *Panoplosaurus*, but most agree it is different. Node lizards (called nodosaurids) were very heavily armored, four-footed dinosaurs. They are known to have lived throughout North America, Europe, and Asia. They probably descended from *Hylaeosaurus* about 125 million years ago. Some scientists think *Hylaeosaurus* was descended from *Scelidosaurus*.

Palaeoscincus was larger than some other node lizards. Scientists believe there were about 19 different types. Some were only 7 feet long. Others were up to 25 feet in length. They walked well above the ground but their heads were low. The neck was short and allowed little movement. Safe inside their bony armor, they would have been troubled by few dinosaurs.

Length: 23 feet
Weight: 3—5 tons
Lived: Late Cretaceous
Found: United States (Montana)

Panoplosaurus
(pan-OP-luh-sawr-us)

Because of its bony plates and protective spikes, this dinosaur was called "fully armored lizard." It was one of the last armored dinosaurs from North America. Its back was protected by hard plates made of bone. Large slabs of bone were attached to its skull. These protected its neck and the sides of its head. Its skin was covered with bony lumps set in the thick skin.

Panoplosaurus had a massive head. It was arched on top and had a narrow snout. This too was covered with bony plates. In its mouth, Panoplosaurus had small teeth with ridges. From the teeth, scientists believe it fed on roots and dug out small bush plants. Dinosaurs like Panoplosaurus were very heavily defended and protected with bony armor. Yet they had weak jaws and poor teeth. They would have spent a lot of time gathering up food with their bony snouts. Protected from attack inside their bony plates and a skin several inches thick, they were little more than eating machines.

Length: 23 feet
Weight: 3—4 tons
Lived: Late Cretaceous
Found: Western North America

Parasaurolophus

(par-ah-sawr-OL-uh-fus)

A large member of the duckbill family of dinosaurs, called hadrosaurids, Parasaurolophus was a close relative of *Lambeosaurus*. Most duckbills were divided into two groups. One had a flat head with no crest. The second group had tall, bony head crests. Each family had a different crest style and families would recognize each other this way. Parasaurolophus had a very special crest. It was a curved, hollow horn that attached to the front of the head and swept backwards.

The horn was more than 6 feet long. Inside, two tubes went up to the top and two came back down. These were breathing tubes. Each pair of tubes going up into the crest was attached to the nostrils in the dinosaur's nose. The down tubes went to the lungs. Scientists have measured the tubes. They believe Parasaurolophus could make a very loud bellowing sound by snorting through these sound tubes.

Length: 33 feet
Weight: 2—4 tons
Lived: Late Cretaceous
Found: United States (Utah, New Mexico), Canada (Alberta)

Pinacosaurus
(pin-AH-kuh-sawr-us)

This dinosaur was called "plank lizard" because it had a heavily armored back. It was a member of the "fused lizard" group, which also included *Ankylosaurus, Euoplocephalus,* and *Sauroplites.* It had a broad mouth and a beak-like face. Its legs were directly below its body and held it off the ground. All members of this family had a big bone club at the end of a long tail. Pinacosaurus had sharp spikes along its back and sides. Bones from this dinosaur have been found in China and Mongolia.

Pinacosaurus was one of the smallest in the "fused lizard" group. It was only half the size of the massive *Ankylosaurus.* It lived in hot, dry climates high above sea level. Food might have been difficult to find where it lived, but it probably went around without challenge. Not many dinosaurs liked very hot places.

Length: 18 feet
Weight: 2 tons
Lived: Late Cretaceous
Found Mongolia, China

Plateosaurus
(PLAY-tee-uh-sawr-us)

This was the most common of the early dinosaurs known to science. Plateosaurus means "flat lizard," and it has given its name to a family of at least seven different types. Others include *Lufengosaurus* and *Massospondylus.* Plateosaurus was larger than either of these. It had a very thick tail with strong muscles. It would have been able to use the base of its spine as a prop. By doing this and rearing up on its hind legs, it could tear down branches of high trees or munch the tops of palms.

These dinosaurs date from the end of the Triassic, more than 200 million years ago. They and their relatives have been found all over the world. Plateosaurus must have been particularly common in Europe, where many fossil bones have been found. These dinosaurs lived for many millions of years before they died out. Some scientists think that they were the true ancestors of the giant, four-footed sauropods like *Apatosaurus* and *Diplodocus.*

Length: 26 feet
Weight: 1 ton
Lived: Late Triassic
Found: Germany, France, Switzerland, England

Podokesaurus
(po-DOE-kee-sawr-us)

This little dinosaur may never have existed. Its name means "swift-footed lizard." Was Podokesaurus a separate animal or was it really a *Coelophysis?* It is known to have lived during the late Triassic or early Jurassic period. It belonged to the family of "hollow form" dinosaurs called coelophysids. Dinosaurs in that group were named after *Coelophysis*. They are known from the skeletons of many animals that lived and died together. It is believed they were all caught by a sudden sandstorm and buried alive. Many dinosaur scientists believe that Podokesaurus was a different animal, but very similar to *Coelophysis*. This little meat eater, alive at the dawn of the dinosaur age, would have stood only 2 feet tall. It was lightly built and had a long tail. It also had long hind legs and a pair of short arms with tiny hands. The bones of this little creature were found in Massachusetts, and no more have been found anywhere else.

Length: 10 feet
Weight: 65 pounds
Lived: Late Triassic
Found: Massachusetts

Prosaurolophus
(pro-sawr-OL-uh-fus)

This dinosaur was the ancestor of *Saurolophus*. It had a sloping face with bumps over the eyebrows. Its mouth was flat and its lower jaw was straight. Prosaurolophus belonged to the family of duckbills that had flat heads or skulls. They did not have large crests or domes on their heads. Prosaurolophus did have a small bony lump that ended in a spike.

Compared to other duckbills, Prosaurolophus was not particularly large. Although some duckbills were only 12 feet long, others, like *Hadrosaurus*, were up to 32 feet in length. Prosaurolophus was 26 feet long, with a strong tail that it usually held straight out behind itself as it loped along on its hind legs. Prosaurolophus laid its eggs in mud mounds shaped like saucers. Some scientists think the adults gathered the young together to look after them. They may even have gathered food for them. Some had flaps of skin that could be blown up like balloons. They may have done this to make loud calls to others in the family.

Length: 26 feet
Weight: 1–4 tons
Lived: Late Cretaceous
Found: Canada (Alberta)

Protoceratops
(pro-toe-SAIR-uh-tops)

About the size of a pig, Protoceratops is the earliest known member of the family of horned dinosaurs. Its name means "first horned face." Many skeletons were discovered by an American expedition to Mongolia in 1922. This expedition also found nests with unhatched baby Protoceratops curled up inside eggs. The baby dinosaurs were only 12 inches long. The eggs were only 6 inches across and had been placed in rows around a bowl-shaped nest. The eggs were separated from each other by layers of sand. These were the first dinosaur eggs to be found.

The closest relatives to Protoceratops were *Bagaceratops* and *Microceratops*. Protoceratops had a large face and a small neck frill. It had a large beak and bumps on its nose and above its eyebrows. These bumps were the first signs of horns that would develop in later dinosaurs. Later horned dinosaurs like *Styracosaurus* and *Triceratops* had big horns and were much larger than Protoceratops.

Length: 6 feet
Weight: 1—2 tons
Lived: Late Cretaceous
Found: Mongolia

Psittacosaurus
(SIT-uh-ko-sawr-us)

Saichania
(sye-CHAY-nee-ah)

Some very good fossil bones of this dinosaur have been found in Mongolia. Its name, which means "beautiful one" in Mongolian, refers to the unusually good state of the fossils and not to the dinosaur's appearance!

Saichania belonged to the late Cretaceous family of armored dinosaurs (ankylosaurids). Members of the same family included *Ankylosaurus*, *Euoplocephalus*, *Pinacosaurus*, *Sauroplites*, and *Tarchia*. Saichania's size was about average for the armored dinosaurs, although much smaller than a huge *Ankylosaurus*.

Saichania had a larger skull than *Pinacosaurus*, with more bumpy bone on top. It had a large number of bone knobs, studs, and spikes in rows across its back and along its tail. Where the back legs were attached to its spine, separate bones were welded together for great strength. The bony club on the end of its tail was similar to the club on *Ankylosaurus*.

This man-sized dinosaur is a member of the "parrot lizard" family. It is linked with the "horned face" dinosaurs. Psittacosaurus looked a bit like *Protoceratops* but had no bone neck frill. It had a beak like a parrot and a deep jaw. Its front legs were quite short, while its back legs were long and very strong. It probably ambled along on all fours and stood on its back legs to reach plants and branches.

Psittacosaurus had four toes on each foot, one of which was a stump like a short thumb. It had four fingers on each hand and claws on each finger and toe. These dinosaurs lived in the early and mid-Cretaceous period. They may have descended from the *Heterodontosaurus* family of the early Jurassic more than 90 million years earlier.

On one bone hunt, scientists found a baby Psittacosaurus only half the size of a pigeon. It is the smallest baby dinosaur found anywhere.

Length: 2 feet, 7 inches to 5 feet
Weight: Up to 50 pounds
Lived: Early Cretaceous
Found: Mongolia, China, USSR (Siberia)

Length: 23 feet
Weight: 2—5 tons
Lived: Late Cretaceous
Found: Mongolia

Saltopus
(SALT-o-pus)

Saurolophus
(sawr-OL-o-fus)

Because it had a large piece of bone sticking out the back of its head, this dinosaur was given the Greek name for "crested lizard." It belonged to the group of "bird foot" dinosaurs and to the family of duckbills. It appeared just as *Corythosaurus* was dying out. It lived at the same times as *Lambeosaurus*. Examples of this dinosaur have been found in North America and Asia. It is a very advanced duckbill and is believed to date back only 75 million years.

Saurolophus looked a lot like *Edmontosaurus*, but it had a long head shaped like a spoon. The dinosaur probably stood 17 feet tall on its back legs and would have reached leaves and branches as high as the roof on a house. It had three hoofed toes on each foot and four webbed fingers on each hand. Two fingers on each hand were also hoofed. Its tail was big and flattened, with strong bones and muscles. This helped the animal control its balance as it shifted from four legs to two. Like all duckbills, it had no teeth in its beak. It did have sets of teeth in its cheeks.

This tiny dinosaur was a member of the "hollow tail" (coelurosaur) family. Because the scientist who discovered it thought it was a jumping dinosaur, he called it Saltopus, which means "leaping foot" in Latin. In fact, Saltopus was probably a fast runner. It is one of the oldest dinosaurs known and was found in a quarry in Scotland during a bone hunt in 1910. Scientists think it fed on small insects and lizards. It was closely related to *Coelophysis* and *Procompsognathus*.

Saltopus had small arms with five fingers on each hand. The fourth and fifth fingers were very small. It had strong muscles at the top of its back legs. These helped it move very fast over rough ground. Saltopus had a pointed face and mouth with rows of small teeth. It was only about the size of a domestic cat and stood 8 inches high at its hip.

Length: 2 feet
Weight: 2 pounds
Lived: Late Triassic
Found: Scotland

Length: 30 feet
Weight: 1—2 tons
Lived: Late Cretaceous
Found: East Asia, North America

Sauroplites
(sawr-uh-PLY-teez)

This is one of the oldest of the "armored dinosaur" (ankylosaur) family and dates back to the early Cretaceous period. Its name means "stone-like lizard" and is taken from the name Hoplite, a heavily armored ancient Greek soldier. Its remains were found on the border between China and Mongolia.

Not many bones of Sauroplites have been found. Enough exist, however, to form a good picture of this early ankylosaur. It is smaller than *Saichania*, another member of the armored family which came much later.

Sauroplites was covered with bony segments set into its skin. It also had plates of bone in rows down its back and on its tail. Bony spikes were attached to the side of its body just behind the neck. These would have given it good protection from the flesh-eating dinosaurs of the Cretaceous period.

Length: 20 feet
Weight: 2 tons
Lived: Early Cretaceous
Found: China

Segisaurus
(SEE-gih-sawr-us)

This very early member of the "hollow-tail lizard" family was probably a descendent of *Coelophysis*. It was about the size of a goose and was found in Arizona. Some scientists have likened it to *Procompsognathus*. However, both *Coelophysis* and *Procompsognathus* had hollow bones, while Segisaurus had solid bones.

Segisaurus was named after Segi Canyon, Arizona, where it was found in 1933. Unfortunately, only parts of the skeleton were found, without a head. This has made it very difficult to build up an accurate picture. The artist here has shown what scientists think its head might have looked like. The animal had long, slim back legs and feet very similar to *Procompsognathus*. These would have helped it run quite fast. Because the teeth have not been found, it is impossible to know precisely what it fed on. However, scientists believe it to have been interested in small lizards and tiny animals.

Remains of Segisaurus continue to puzzle scientists. The back-jutting hipbones have tiny holes in them, and the animal has a collarbone. The collarbone had almost disappeared in dinosaurs, even the early ones. Apart from its feet, there were other similarities between Segisaurus and *Procompsognathus*. The hipbones were almost identical, and the arm bones looked as though they belonged to the same family. Much of the work of comparing Segisaurus with *Procompsognathus* was carried out by Professor John Ostrom in 1981.

Length: 3 feet, 4 inches
Weight: 20 pounds
Lived: Early Jurassic
Found: United States (Arizona)

Shanshanosaurus
(shan-SHAN-uh-sawr-us)

This small dinosaur was found by fossil hunters in China. So far, this is the only specimen that has been discovered. The skeleton was built of very thin bones for light weight and flexibility. Its name is taken from the Shan-shan area of China, where it was found. A close relative, called *Noasaurus*, was found in Argentina. Each was like a cross between *Deinonychus* and *Dromaeosaurus*. *Noasaurus* had a terrifying claw on each foot like *Deinonychus*, but it was flexible and more sharply curved.

Shanshanosaurus had a large head shaped like a wedge. Its teeth were very sharp and its eyes were small. No doubt it had poor eyesight. It had a long neck, short arms, and long, muscular legs. On them, this fierce little predator could have moved fast across rough ground. It probably fed on small plant eaters or baby dinosaurs, such as the young of *Diplodocus* and *Apatosaurus*. Only big meat eaters like *Tyrannosaurus* could have gone after fully grown plant eaters. Dinosaurs like Shanshanosaurus probably had to make do with smaller animals.

Length: 6 feet
Weight: 25–30 pounds
Lived: Late Cretaceous
Found: China

Shantungosaurus
(shan-TUNG-o-sawr-us)

With a flat head and a huge body, Shantungosaurus is easily the biggest duckbill yet discovered. It turned up in Shantung, China, and belongs to the large family of hadrosaurine duckbills. It is closely related to *Edmontosaurus*, *Hadrosaurus*, *Maiasaura*, *Prosaurolophus*, and *Saurolophus*. Some members of the family may have been up to 50 feet long and stood 25 feet high. Shantungosaurus had a low skull with a flat top to its head, a flat beak, and no crest, as did some hadrosaurids.

Shantungosaurus was very similar to *Edmontosaurus* but much bigger. It dates from the late Cretaceous period and would have been an impressive sight. A full-scale reconstruction has been set up at the Natural History Museum in Beijing, the capital city of China. A full-grown man standing beside the reconstruction only comes up to the dinosaur's knee. Were it in existence today, Shantungosaurus would be looking over the tops of three-story houses!

Length: 39–49 feet
Weight: 3–4 tons
Lived: Late Cretaceous
Found: China

Spinosaurus
(SPY-nuh-sawr-us)

Several dinosaurs and other animals had large spines on their backs covered with skin. This gave these animals the appearance of having sails on their backs. *Ouranosaurus* was one. Spinosaurus is another. Both lived in the early Cretaceous. Spinosaurus was large and carried 6-foot spines on its back. Both *Ouranosaurus* and Spinosaurus were found from remains discovered in Africa. Skeletons of Spinosaurus also show it to have been a meat eater. It had teeth serrated like steak knives, but they were straight and not curved like those of some other dinosaurs.

Spinosaurus has been put in a group called spinosaurids. The group included several families, among them Altispinax. They were large carnivores and hunted widely for food and prey. The sail may have helped them warm up more quickly than other dinosaurs by taking in heat from the sun. This would have been an advantage when they set out hunting.

Length: 40 feet
Weight: 7 tons
Lived: Late Cretaceous
Found: Niger, Egypt

Staurikosaurus
(stor-IK-uh-sawr-us)

This dinosaur belongs in a family of its own. It has no known relatives. It is, however, part of a group of families known as prosauropods, or "before the lizard-feet dinosaurs." They included the first of the big, four-footed plant eaters like *Plateosaurus* as well as smaller, lighter animals like *Thecodontosaurus*.

Staurikosaurus was named after the Southern Cross, a group of stars best seen in the southern hemisphere. Staurikosaurus was found in southern Brazil. They were among the very first dinosaurs and are known to have existed more than 210 million years ago.

Dinosaurs of this family walked and ran on two legs but could have dropped to all fours if necessary. They had large heads, compact bodies, and sharp teeth. They had five fingers on each hand and five toes on each foot. The middle toes and fingers were the longest.

Length: 6 feet, 6 inches
Weight: Up to 66 pounds
Lived: Middle Triassic
Found: Brazil (Santa Maria)

Stegosaurus
(STEG-uh-sawr-us)

Stegosaurus was first discovered in 1877 from bones found in Colorado. Nobody really knows why it had such big, bony plates on its back. Some scientists think they were there to radiate excess heat from the animal's body. Others believe they were a protection from flesh-eating dinosaurs. Stegosaurus was closely related to 'Kentrosaurus, Lexovisaurus, and Tuojiangosaurus. Its name means "plated lizard" and refers to all the plates, spikes, and spines on its back and tail.

Stegosaurus had a very small, tube-like head, small teeth, and a brain the size of a walnut. Nevertheless, it could defend itself by lashes from armored spikes on its tail. Its front legs were only half the length of its back legs. The dinosaur probably munched small plants and tree roots, nibbling leaves from small trees or foliage from bushes. Many Stegosaurus bones have been found in Oklahoma, Utah, and Wyoming. Others have turned up in Europe, Africa, India, and China.

Length: 30 feet
Weight: 2 tons
Lived: Late Jurassic
Found: United States (Colorado, Wyoming, Oklahoma, Utah)

Stenonychosaurus
(sten-ON-ik-uh-sawr-us)

If brain size is an indication of intelligence, Stenonychosaurus must have been one of the most intelligent dinosaurs to exist. With a large brain and huge eyes, it was very similar to Saurornithoides, its relative. In other ways, it was like the family of Dromaeosaurus. It had a long, stiffened tail, long arms, a second toe with a claw, and strong back legs. It also had wide-set eyes for good focusing. It would have judged distance well. Clearly, Stenonynchosaurus was agile, quick-moving, and quick-thinking. It probably stalked its prey like many animals do today. Most dinosaurs survived by instinct. Stenonynchosaurus could get the better of its prey by using brain power to respond to its developed senses. These included sight, sound, and smell. It probably had fast reflexes and could dart about at great speed. Fossil remains have been found in Canada, and they date back about 80 million years.

Length: 6 feet, 6 inches
Weight: 60 to 100 pounds
Lived: Late Cretaceous
Found: Canada (Alberta)

Struthiomimus
(strooth-ee-uh-MY-mus)

Because scientists thought this dinosaur looked like an ostrich, they called it Struthiomimus, which means "ostrich mimic." It had a short body, a long tail, and a curving neck. Its head was small, it had no teeth, and its eyes were quite large. Scientists think that it may have been fairly intelligent, compared to most other dinosaurs. Struthiomimus probably lived on open river banks, pacing around for a juicy morsel. It might have caught some of the many kinds of water life that lived in the late Cretaceous. Perhaps instead it used its strong, curved claws to tear open insect nests or eggs.

This dinosaur was a member of the family of *Ornithomimus*, which belonged to the broad group of "hollow-tail lizards," or coelurosaurs. Other members of the family included *Dromiceiomimus*, *Elaphrosaurus*, and *Gallimimus*.

Length: 11 feet, 6 inches
Weight: 220 pounds
Lived: Late Cretaceous
Found: United States (New Jersey), Canada (Alberta)

Styracosaurus
(sty-RAK-uh-sawr-us)

This is one of the most dramatic members of the short-frilled, "horned dinosaur" family. It was related to *Brachyceratops*, *Centrosaurus*, *Ceratops*, *Eoceratops*, *Monoclonius*, *Pachyrhinosaurus*, and *Triceratops*. Each of these animals had a different arrangement of horns and frills made of bone. Seen from head on, as pictured on the front of this book, Styracosaurus was a fearsome beast. It had a long head with six large spikes that were attached to the back of its neck frill. There was a long horn on its nose and a curved beak for tearing stubborn roots or tree trunks.

Styracosaurus was probably about 6 feet tall and would have weighed around 3 tons. Scientists have calculated that it could have reached a speed of more than 20 MPH in full charge. In some ways it was the equivalent of today's rhinoceros, but much stronger and more dangerous. For all its frightening appearance, however, it was little more than half the size of *Triceratops*.

Length: 18 feet
Weight: 1—2 tons
Lived: Late Cretaceous
Found: United States (Montana), Canada (Alberta)

Syntarsus
(sin-TAR-sus)

This strange dinosaur was found in southern Africa. It dates back to the earliest period of the dinosaur age. Most pieces of the skeleton were found, and experts have put together a good picture of how it must have looked. The bones in its hands look similar to those from *Coelophysis*, and the two lived at about the same time. Syntarsus's foot bones, however, look more like those from a member of the *Heterodontosaurus* family. Its ankle bones look very primitive. They are fused together and not well developed.

Scientists wanted to show dinosaurs with feathers and plumes on their heads, so they drew pictures of Syntarsus this way. Today, very few scientists think it had those features. It would have been surprising to have found feathers on a member of the Coelophysis family. Syntarsus had sharp teeth in its pointed mouth. It was probably quite fast and could run after small mammals and large insects.

Length: 10 feet
Weight: 65 pounds
Lived: Late Triassic
Found: Zimbabwe

Teratosaurus
(teh-RAT-uh-sawr-us)

Members of this family were the first of the big meat-eating carnosaurs, or "flesh lizards." They emerged around 200 million years ago, at the dawn of the dinosaur age. About 100 million years later, the big carnosaurs like *Tenontosaurus* and *Tyrannosaurus* would appear to scavenge the earth. Dinosaurs like Teratosaurus, however, were much faster and more agile than their giant, lumbering descendents. Teratosaurus was found in West Germany. Others from the same family have been found in England and Africa.

Teratosaurus had a large head, a strong neck, and a short body. It had fangs in its mouth and claws on its fingers and toes. Each arm had three fingers and each foot had four toes. Compare this arrangement with dinosaurs like *Tyrannosaurus* and *Tenontosaurus*, which had almost lost the use of their arms.

Length: 20 feet
Weight: 1,500 pounds
Lived: Late Triassic
Found: West Germany, England, Africa

Triceratops
(try-SAIR-uh-tops)

Along with giant meat eaters like *Tyrannosaurus*, Triceratops is probably one of the most famous dinosaurs ever found. It has been fully examined by scientists, thanks to the discovery of a large bed of skeletons in western Wyoming. Along with *Torosaurus*, Triceratops is one of the last of the large group of horned dinosaurs called ceratopsians. Its name comes from the Greek name for three large horns.

Triceratops had a relatively short frill, especially when compared with that of *Torosaurus*. The frill had no holes to make the bone lighter, as some others did. It did have small bumpy pieces of bone on the back edge of the frill. The skull and frill together span a length of more than 6 feet. The two main horns are each more than 3 feet long.

Animals of this family would have been well-protected by their thick, leathery skin and their bony head decoration. They were probably quite slow-moving and would have used their horns more for wrestling than for charging their enemy.

Length: 30 feet
Weight: 6 tons
Lived: Late Cretaceous
Found: United States (Montana, Wyoming, South Dakota), Canada (Alberta)

Tsintaosaurus
(chin-TAY-o-sawr-us)

This was one of the last of the crested duckbills to appear on earth before all dinosaurs became extinct. Very unusual, it is of particular interest to scientists. It was found in China, and its name means "Chinese lizard." Some people think Tsintaosaurus was a descendent of *Sauroplophus*. The bony knob on the top of a *Sauroplophus* skull looks like a primitive form of the main crest on Tsintaosaurus.

Because its crest is so unusual, scientists want to know if it was used for show or developed by nature for fighting. The crest is known to have been a hollow tube. Many crested dinosaurs had hollow tubes that were probably used for making loud, booming sounds. Tsintaosaurus may have had a flap of skin stretching from its beak to the top of the crest. This would have been for show. Many animals develop parts of their body for frightening away enemies or attracting other members of their kind.

Length: 33 feet
Weight: 4 tons
Lived: Late Cretaceous
Found: China

Tyrannosaurus
(tye-RAN-uh-sawr-us)

This is certainly the biggest meat eater and may have been the most frightening dinosaur. It was more than 40 feet long and would have stood more than 18 feet tall on its huge back legs. Its strong tail probably helped balance the animal as it lunged forward and crashed into its prey. Its head was massive and very strong. In the specimens available, some back bones were welded together. This would have resulted from collisions to the head, which then sent enormous shocks down its back. Before the bones welded, the dinosaur would have suffered terrible pain from arthritis.

With legs like giant pillars, Tyrannosaurus would have had a top speed of nearly 20 MPH. It could have kept up this pace for only short distances, though. Probably, it lay in wait for easy prey and gave a short chase. After finally crashing into its next meal, it stunned it with a massive blow from its head. Then Tyrannosaurus would kill its prey with a bone-crushing bite from its huge jaws. Its 3-foot jaws held 60 teeth, each shaped like a dagger and up to 6 inches in length.

Length: 39 feet
Weight: 7 tons
Lived: Late Cretaceous
Found: Western North America

Velociraptor
(veh-loss-ih-RAP-tor)

Velociraptor means "swift plunderer," and this dinosaur was very likely just that. Lightly built for speed and agility, it had a long, low head and a flat skull. Although some of its relatives, including *Dromaeosaurus* and *Deinonychus*, have been found in North America, Velociraptor comes from Mongolia. The shape of its head and mouth suggests that it was a variety of coelurosaur ("hollow-tailed lizard") that developed around the diet it got. One skeleton has been found with its hands clutching the head of a *Protoceratops*. Both dinosaurs seemed to have died in this final fight to the end.

Velociraptor had long fingers, each with a large claw. This would have made it efficient at killing its prey before eating it. Each foot had four toes. The "big" toe was turned in, the first toe had a large claw and the other two were used for standing on. It could run quite fast and probably lived and hunted alone.

Length: 6 feet
Weight: ?
Lived: Late Cretaceous
Found: Mongolia, China

TERMS TO REMEMBER

Ankylosaurs   "Fused lizard" dinosaurs with heavy bodies, short limbs and protective armor.

Carnosaurs   Means "flesh lizard"; the large and powerful flesh-eating dinosaurs.

Ceratopsian   "Horned dinosaurs", which were among the last to appear and among the most abundant of all dinosaur groups. A type with large beaks and neck frills.

Coelurosaurs   Means "hollow-tailed lizard"; a group of 16 separate dinosaur families, all of which were small and slightly built.

Cretaceous   The most recent period of the Mesozoic, generally considered to have begun 135 million years ago and to have ended 65 million years ago.

**

Fossil   A remnant, impression, or trace of an animal or plant of past geological ages, preserved in the Earth's crust.

Gondwanaland   The Southern Continent that resulted when Pangaea split up in the late Triassic period. This land mass later split again to form South America, Africa, India, Antarctica, and Australia.

Hadrosaurid   A category of duck-billed, plant-eating dinosaurs with a hollow crest on its head, which enhanced its sense of smell.

Herbivore   Any plant-eating creature.

**

Jurassic   The middle period of the Mesozoic, generally considered to have begun 190 million years ago and to have ended 135 million years ago.

Laurasia   The Northern Continent that resulted when Pangaea split up in the late Triassic period. This land mass later split again to form North America, Europe, and Asia.

Mammals   A class of higher vertebrates including man and other animals that nourish their young with milk secreted by mammary glands and are usually more or less covered with hair.

Mesozoic	Comes from the Greek meaning "middle life" and refers to the geologic period between the Paleozoic and the Cenozoic. The Mesozoic is divided into three periods; the Triassic, the Jurassic and the Cretaceous.
Ornithopods	"Bird feet" dinosaurs capable of walking on their back legs.
Ornithischian	One of two families of dinosaur which means "bird-hipped" animal.
Paleontology	The science of dealing with past life from early geologic records and fossil remains.
Pangaea	The supercontinent that contained all of the Earth's land masses in pre-Mesozoic times.
Phytosaurs	The earliest known flesh-eaters, these creatures were among the first dinosaurs of the early Triassic period.
Prosauropods	Means literally "before the lizard feet" dinosaurs, or Sauropods.
Proterosuchians	Enormous, heavy creatures which evolved from the pre-dinosaur reptiles known as the Thecodontians.
Pseudosuchians	Lighter, more nimble descendants of the Proterosuchians, which evolved from the early Triassic reptiles known as the Thecodontians, ancestors of the dinosaurs.
Pterosaurs	Bird-like "winged lizards" which were not dinosaurs at all but a group of animals capable of gliding long distances.
Quetzalcoatlus	The largest flying creature that ever lived. This Pterosaur had a wingspan of 39 feet.
Reptiles	Animals that crawl or move on their belly or on short legs. The body is usually covered with scales or bony plates.
Saurischian	One of two families of dinosaur which means "lizard-hipped" animal.
Sauropods	The family of "lizard-feet" dinosaurs which included some of the largest animals known to have lived.
Stegosaurs	"Roof lizard", or plated dinosaurs with bones or spikes protruding through thick skin.
Thecodontians	Socket-toothed reptiles which first appeared about 230 million years ago and are thought to have given way to the dinosaurs.
Triassic	The earliest period of the Mesozoic, generally considered to have begun 225 million years ago and ended 190 million yeas ago.